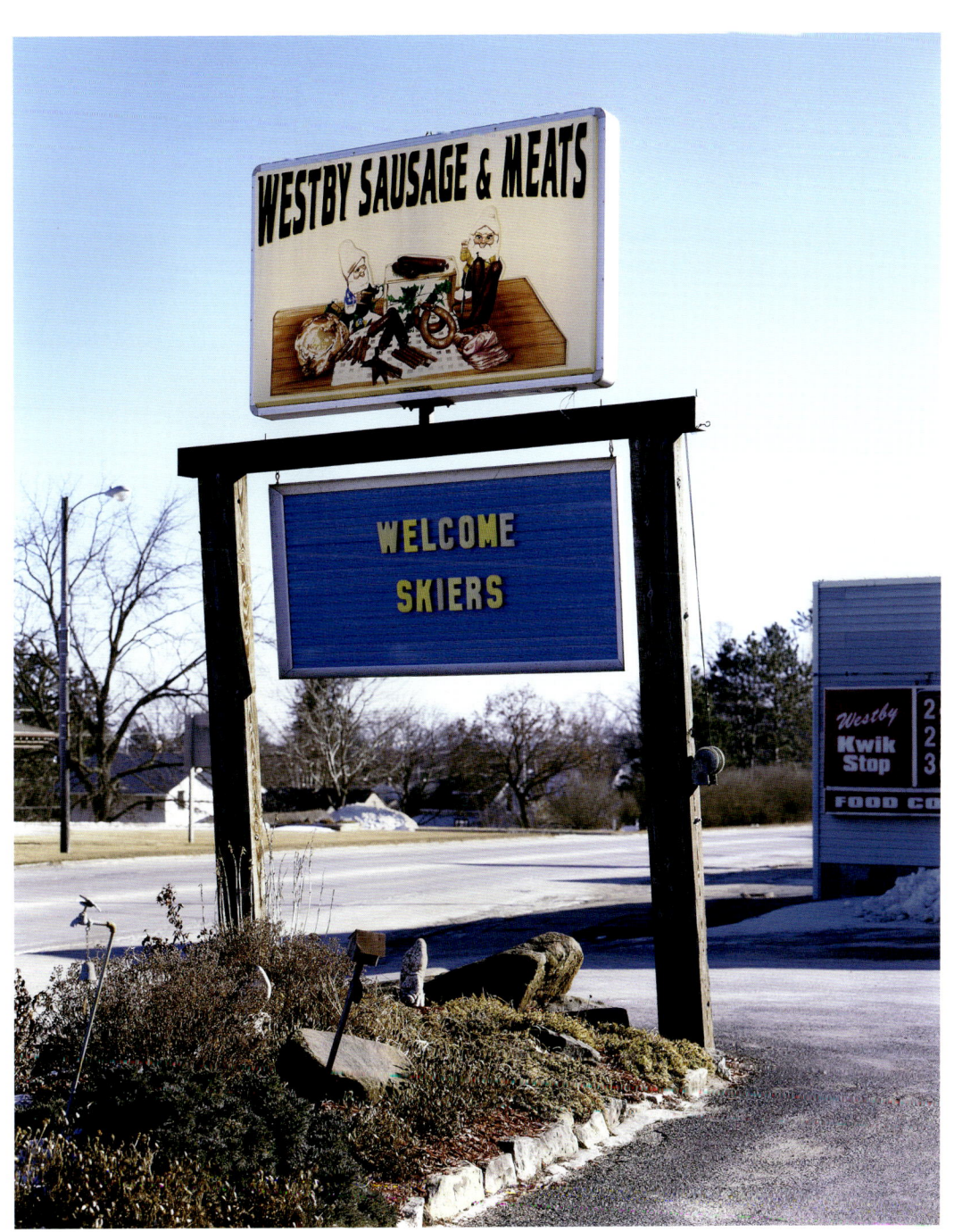

Cofounders: Taj Forer and Michael Itkoff
Creative Director: Ursula Damm

© 2019 Daylight Community Arts Foundation

Photographs © 2019 Cooper Dodds
The Memory of Flight © 2019 Peter Geye
Reflections on the Ghosts of Place © 2019 Chris Lamb

ISBN 978-1-942084-76-1

Printed by Artron, China

Daylight Books
E-mail: info@daylightbooks.org
Web: www.daylightbooks.org

Flying in the Heartland

Jumper

Cooper Dodds

Daylight

The Memory of Flight

By Peter Geye

My ski jumping memories reside in a ghost ski jump, one that used to rise from the side of the tenth fairway on the Theodore Wirth golf course in Minneapolis. That was where my father took me on a Saturday morning when I was seven years old to try the sport for the first time, and it's the first place I visit any time my mind drifts back to the cold winter mornings that were the defining feature of my youth.

My first coach was a patient Norwegian named Selmer Swanson, who, by 1978, had coached thousands of kids through his program at Wirth Park. We met in the golf club locker room, where he fitted an old pair of jumping boots on my feet and had me practice falling from a bench into a telemark landing on the floor. Soon after, he picked a pair of Kongsberg skis from his storeroom and sent me outside to try them. I remember my abiding fear, and Selmer's steady backing, and later that first morning, clipping my boots into bindings and letting my skis run down a snow-covered hill for the first time. The buzz remains with me even now, over forty years later.

There were probably a dozen kids who practiced at Wirth, and our camaraderie was on par with the joy of the sport. We laughed and crashed and were buoyed by Selmer's words of encouragement. He was more concerned with the telemark than he was with how far we went, and those jumps that didn't include the requisite landing were softly critiqued. Those of us who had trouble were cheered on by our friends, and though we were competitors—a contest was held each Saturday, with nickle-size medals in gold, silver, and bronze the cherished prizes—we were, even more, a brotherhood. I

can recall with clarity and certainty the pride we all felt in each other. Win or lose.

I'm also certain that if you put the bunch of us on barstools today, the twelve of us would remember those mornings with equal measures of fondness and sincerity. We'd call up the crosswinds that stalked us and the cold that swiped at our faces. We'd reminisce about the icy inruns and hard-as-steel landing hills, and the knob bonking, a term reserved for especially short jumps. And surely we'd joke about the crashes we avoided, and the ones we didn't. But we'd also recall the favorable headwinds and the bliss they ensured, and the sweet landings at the bottom of the hill, a place we called the pit. We'd talk about tournaments won and lost, dreams we still wake from, and friendships immune from the ravages of time.

So too, I'm sure, would any other dozen jumpers—from Hanover, New Hampshire, to Steamboat Springs, Colorado, to Anchorage, Alaska—for there's no such thing as a ski jumper who doesn't want to get together with compatriots to gab about the good old days.

But I'm just as happy to play those memories back in solitude, something I often do. I spent twelve years jumping, twelve winters that formed in me the closest thing to a devout faith I'll ever know. The memories are permanent. They unfurl over and over again, and I visit them as a way of finding peace and quiet in the tumult of daily life.

As I got older, I got better, and the relatively small jumps at Wirth Park weren't enough hill. By the time I was thirteen or fourteen, I traveled all over the Midwest, to competitions that sometimes had upwards of a hundred kids in them. Big Chester in Duluth; the Hidden Valley jump in Ely; Harrington Hill in St. Paul. Big Bush, Wolverine, Silvermine, Bulldozer and his big brother in Iron Mountain, and of course, Suicide Hill. The names are as easily recalled as the friends who were there with me. So is the memory of arriving at a new jump on any given weekend, and the sense of awe merely driving up to them. It was thrilling, then as now.

Almost all those jumps rose above small towns, their iron or wood scaffolds like lodestars on state highways or county roads. They were places where communities gathered to find common purpose. Even pride. Some of the ski clubs that took care of these jumps—that built and repaired them, undertook the labors of readying them for use, and cultivated the jumpers to fly from them—were close to a century old even when I was a kid.

But not all of them are still around. Big Chester is gone. So is the jump at Hidden Valley in Ely, having been relocated to the Norge Ski Club in Chicago. Big Bush was torn down and replaced. The jump at Wirth Park—the jump of my childhood—disappeared soon after I started college. What's left are the memories and stories, told on barstools and around bonfires with cold cans of Old Style beer, and a common devoutness. Old and young people alike, each of us with our religion.

But the jumps that remain, the Midwestern giants, had then, as they do now, something akin to their own wisdom. It's born of standing tall in the long, dark winters, and of harboring so many years of exhilaration, joy, and fear. In this way, the jumps are the perfect meeting and holding places for those of us predisposed to nostalgia and its stories. I remember a nearly perfect jump one morning on Silvermine, in Eau Claire, Wisconsin, when I was sixteen years old. I went farther than I'd ever gone in my life, and when I got to the end of the outrun and looked up at the jump silhouetted against the clouds, I felt a calmness I'd never known before. I can also recall my first jump on the big hill at Westby later that season. It was my first ride on a 90-meter jump. The inrun was sheer ice, without a track, and even the best skiers were having a hard time with it. My coach told me all I had to do was stay forward, which I did, and it took until I was in flight to realize I'd made it. I can still feel the pressure beneath my skis, and leading with my chin as I pulled myself forward. That was the first day I felt like I wasn't a kid anymore. These are but two of hundreds of recollections, some worn into my muscle memory, others as faint as a sun dog in northern Minnesota. I couldn't live without them.

In early 2019, as I sat at my desk researching a novel I've been trying to write for years—one about ski jumping, one that's already hundreds of pages long, one that's foiled me time and time again, probably because of my long memory—I got an email from a former coach asking if I'd be willing to talk to another former ski jumper about a book of photographs he was going to publish. The serendipity was striking, and I couldn't pass up the opportunity.

That former ski jumper was Cooper Dodds, and the book he was putting together is the one you hold in your hands.

I think these pictures, striking and strange in the best way, capture Midwestern ski jumping communities in a way that makes plain in images what I've been trying to convey in words for years. Whether the shots are of jumpers, serene in flight, or of the steely jumps, enduring against the winter sky and long, interminable landscape, they capture the essence of our sport: We are a community of souls endeavoring together to capture what can only be truly experienced alone—the ecstasy of flight, and the nervousness and danger that accompanies it in this sport.

The five ski jumps shot here have persevered against time and neglect and the hard Midwestern winters. You can still see them, should you find yourself driving down state highways or on county roads up in Ishpeming, Eau Claire, Fox River Grove, Westby, or through my part of the Midwest up in Minneapolis. If you're there at exactly the right time, you can see them lit up under the night sky, bedecked for the infrequent competitions. And if you stop during one of those tournaments, you might catch a jumper letting go of the starting bar and schussing down the inrun. You might see them launch into a flight that won't ever end. Not after they land in a telemark. Not after they get to the end of the outrun and come to a stop and unclip their bindings and hoist their skis up onto their shoulders. Not after they pack up their gear and head home. Not even after years go by.

And though their flights travel with them, they stay behind, too. In the pine forests of Michigan's upper peninsula or the coulees of southern Wisconsin, in the suburbs of Chicago or Minneapolis, they haunt these hallowed places like whispered prayers. These photographs are of contemporary jumpers, but you can see in their faces the quiet longing that will be there in even greater abundance in forty years. You can see in their flight simple grace. And you can see in the jumps themselves that they're holy places.

I've worshipped at all of them, and sometimes still do. But my solemnest thoughts return to Wirth Park and the beginning of it all. The hill that rises up on the edge of the tenth fairway is overgrown with trees now, but it doesn't take any imagination at all to see the old jump there. I visit it often. I can still hear Selmer telling me not to forget my telemark landing, and any of a dozen friends telling me to have a good one before I kick into the track. I was flying then. I still am.

Peter Geye is the award-winning author of three novels, including *Wintering*, *The Lighthouse Road*, and *Safe from the Sea*. He was born and raised in Minneapolis, where he learned to ski jump when he was seven years old. He holds a PhD from Western Michigan University and an MFA from the University of New Orleans, and is a regular teaching artist at The Loft in Minneapolis.

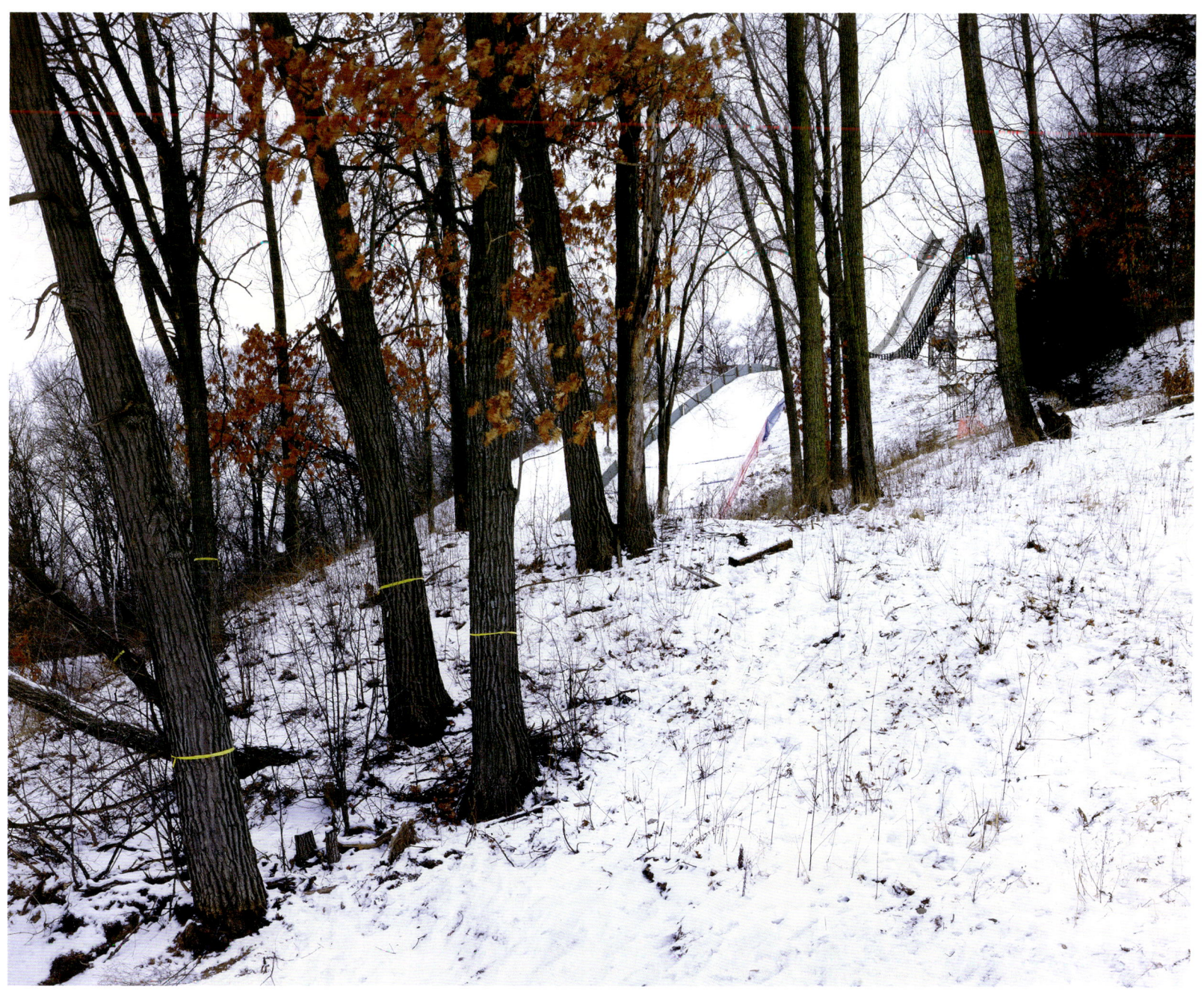

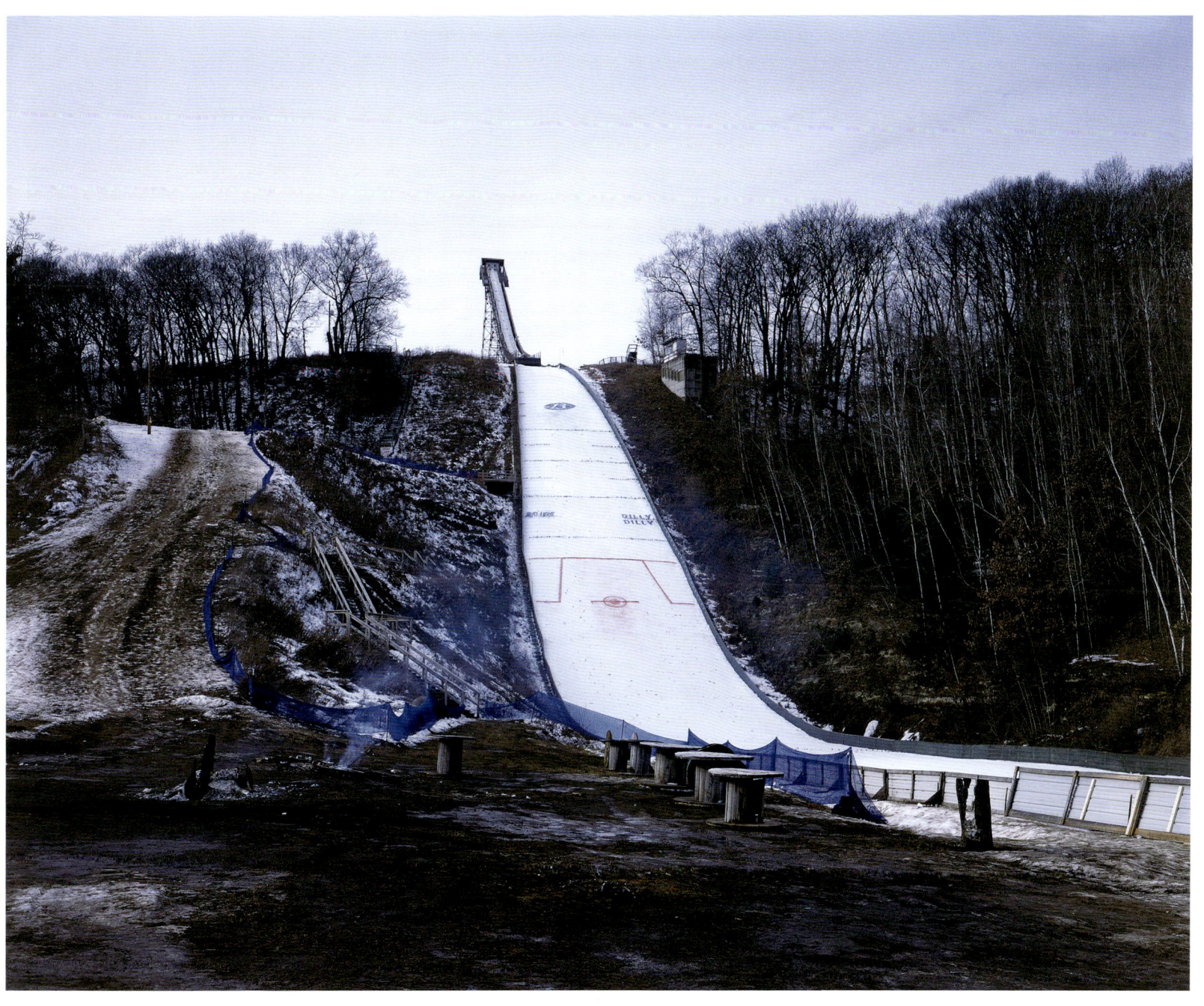

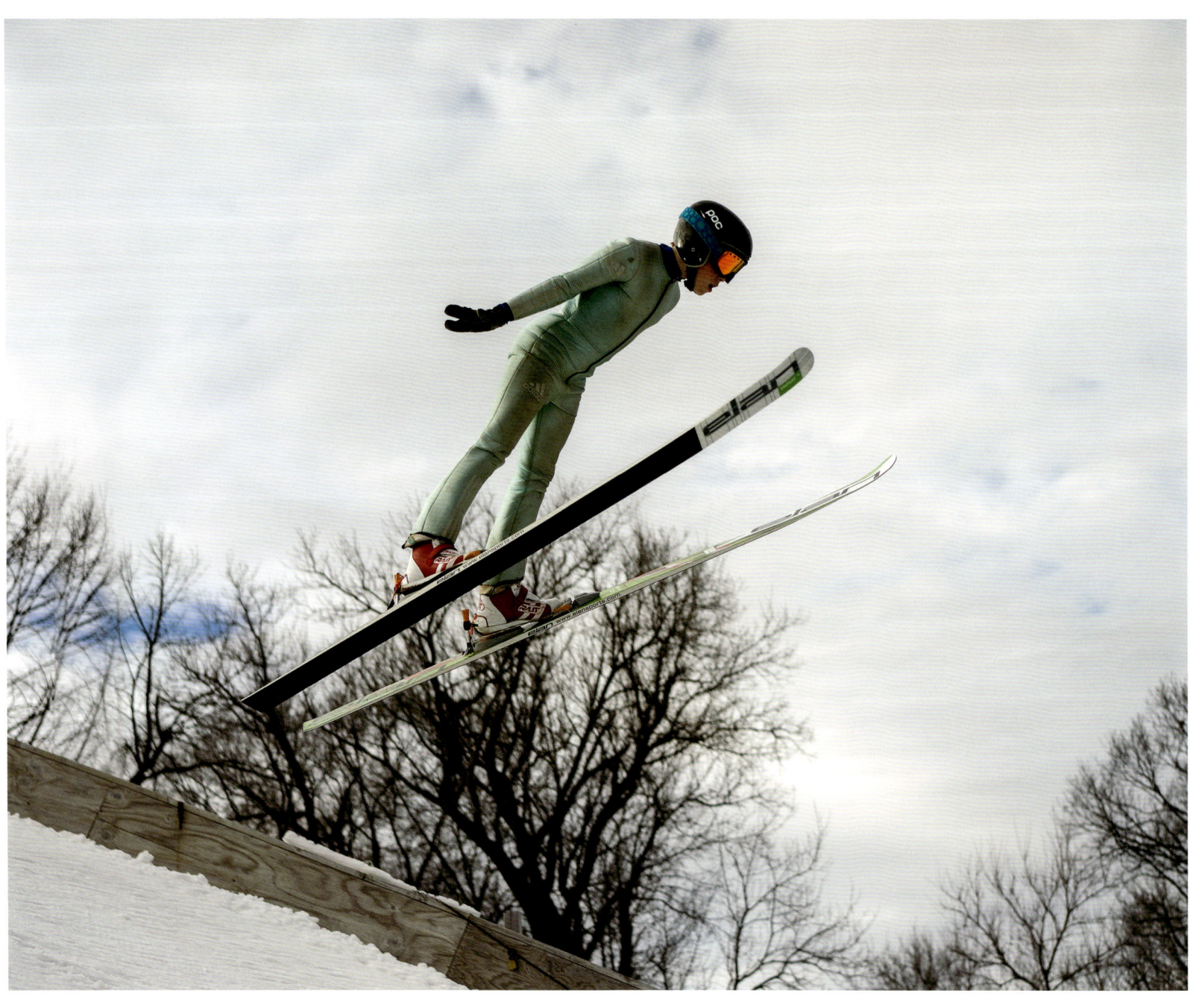

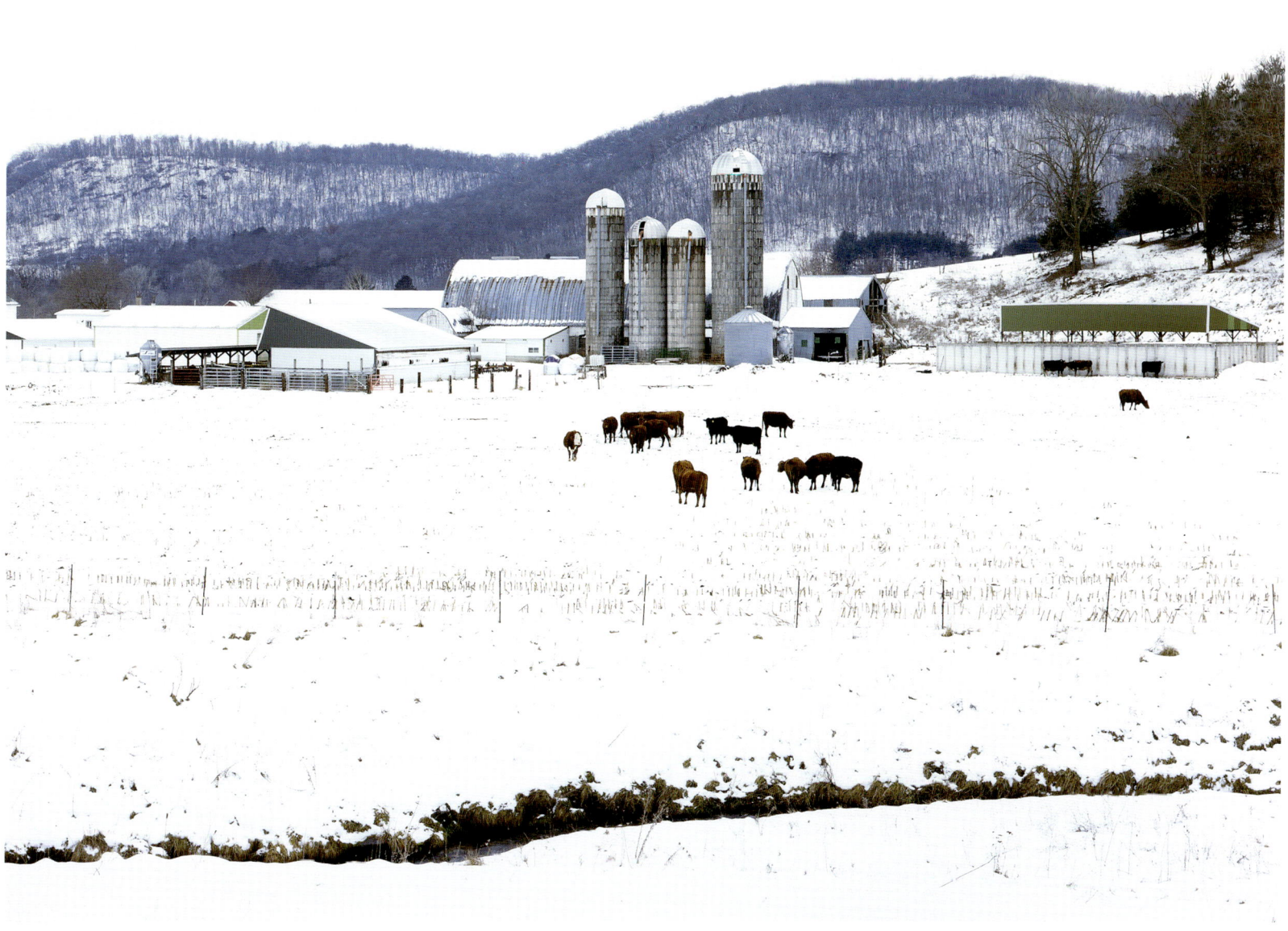

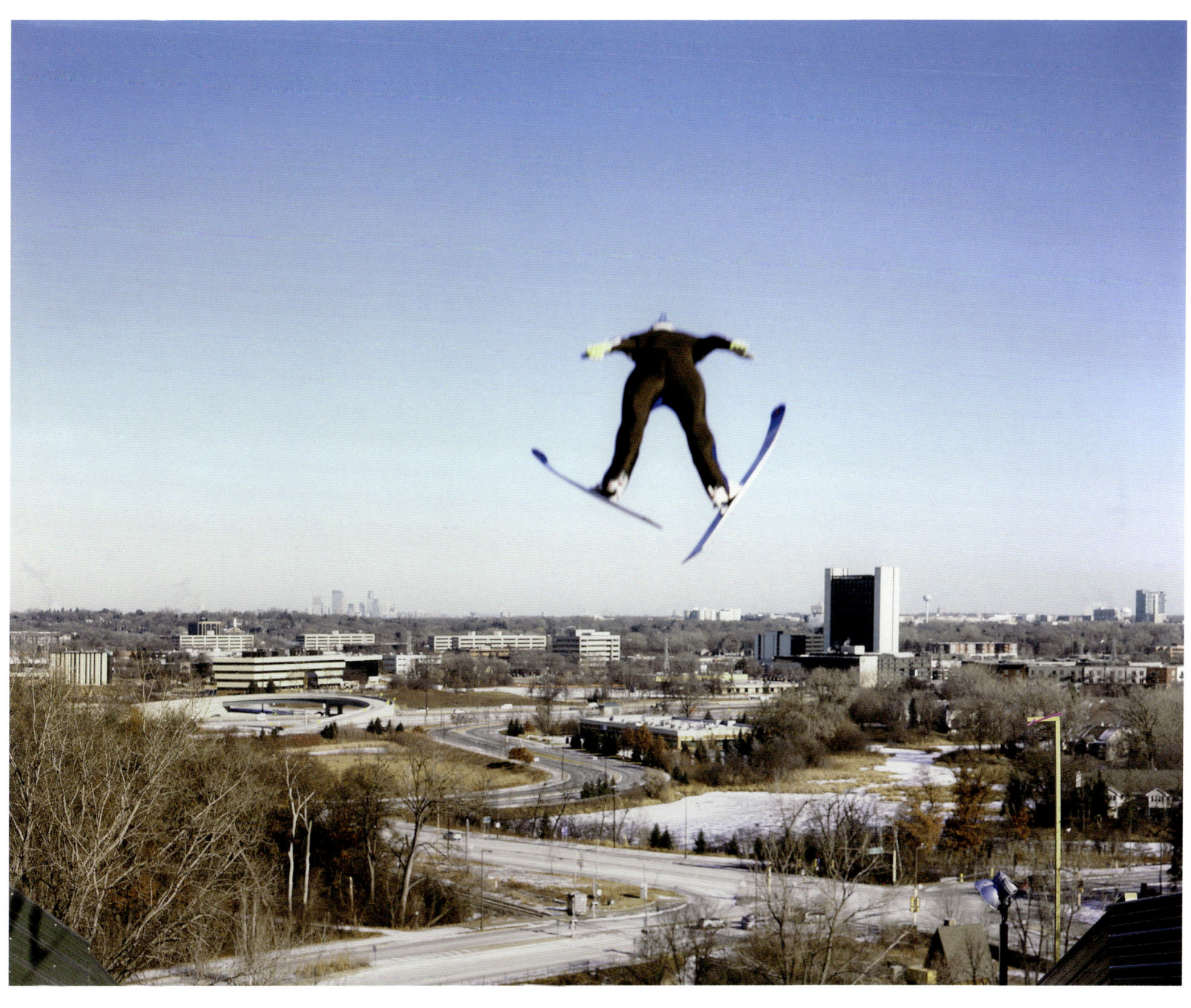

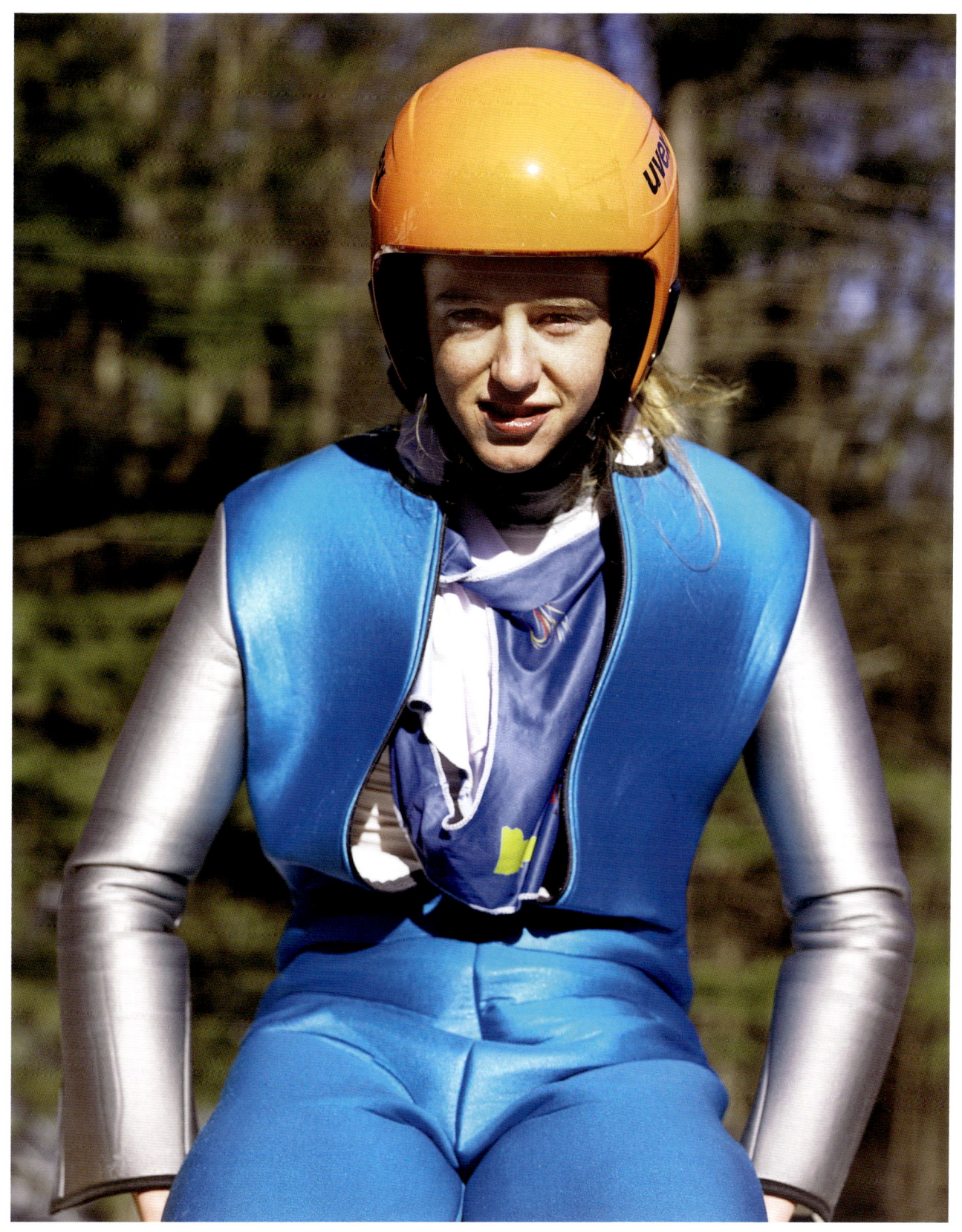

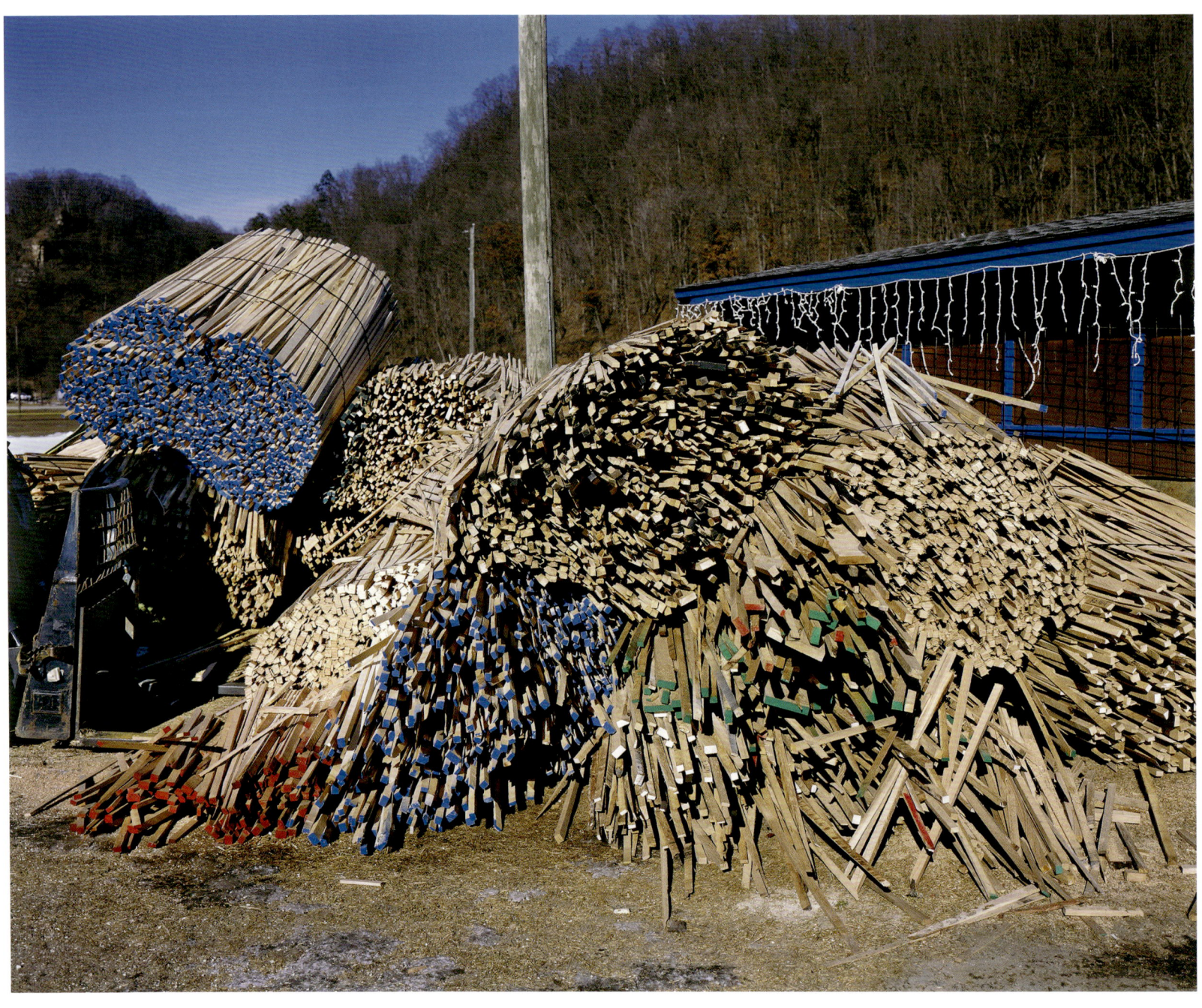

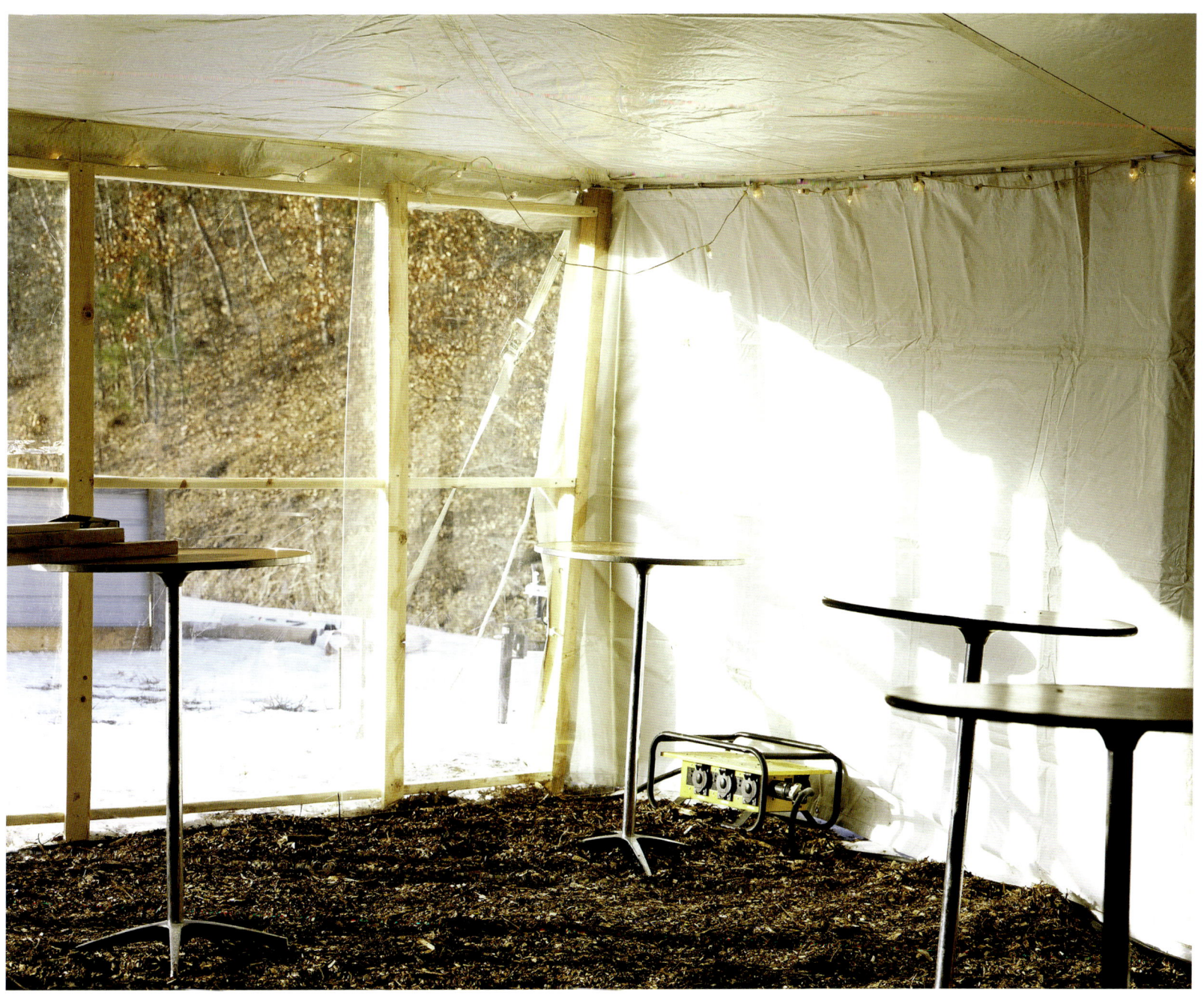

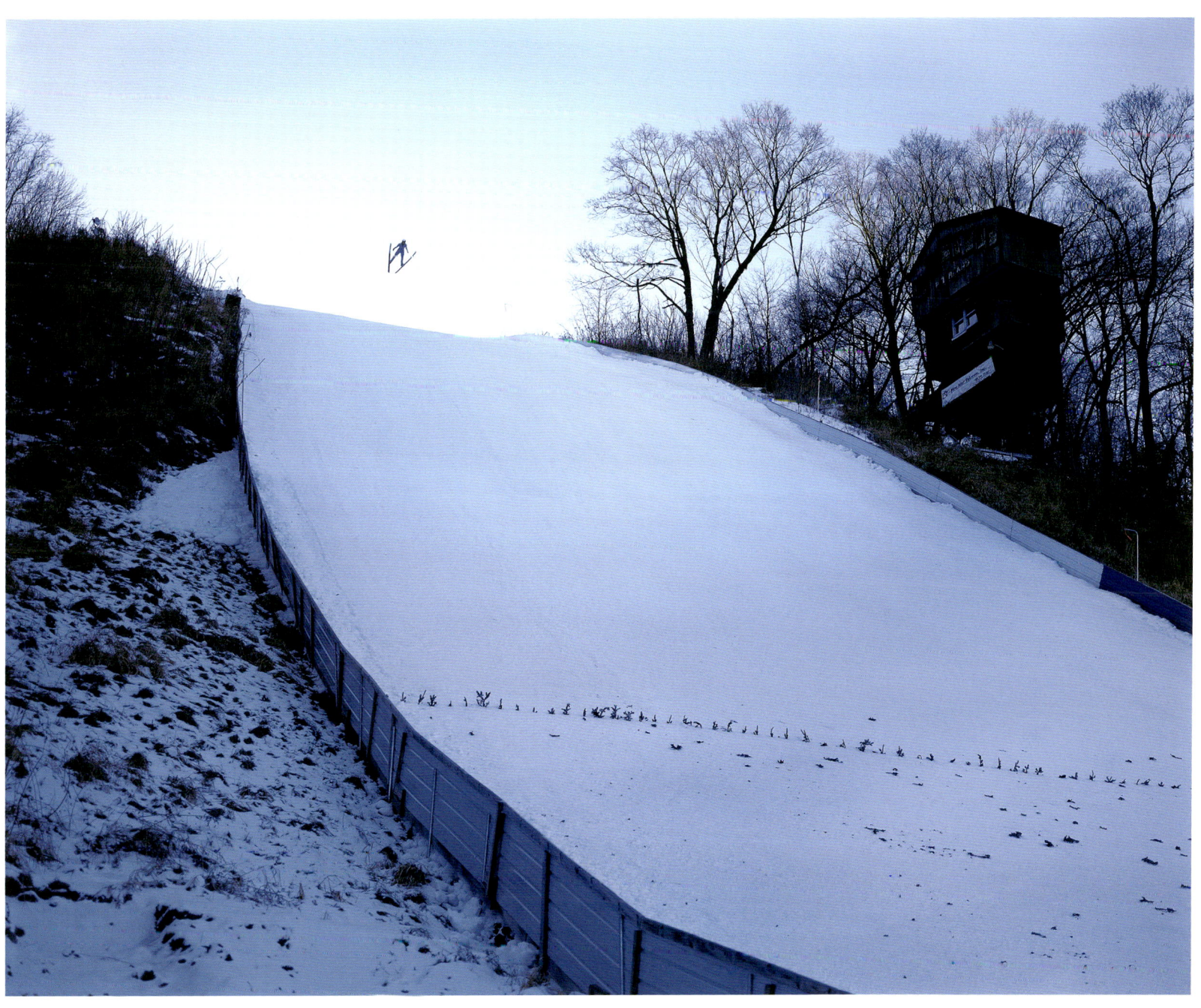

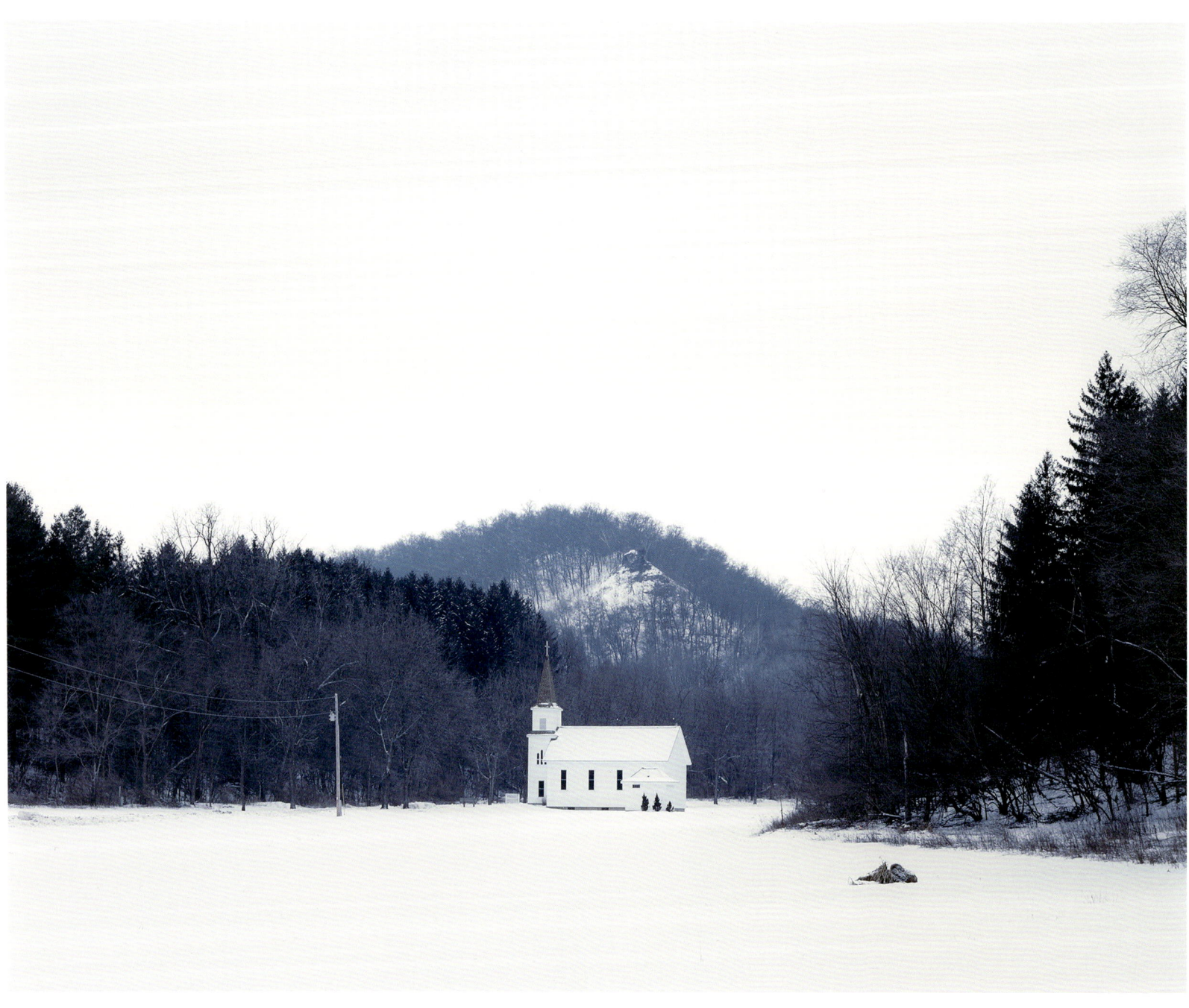

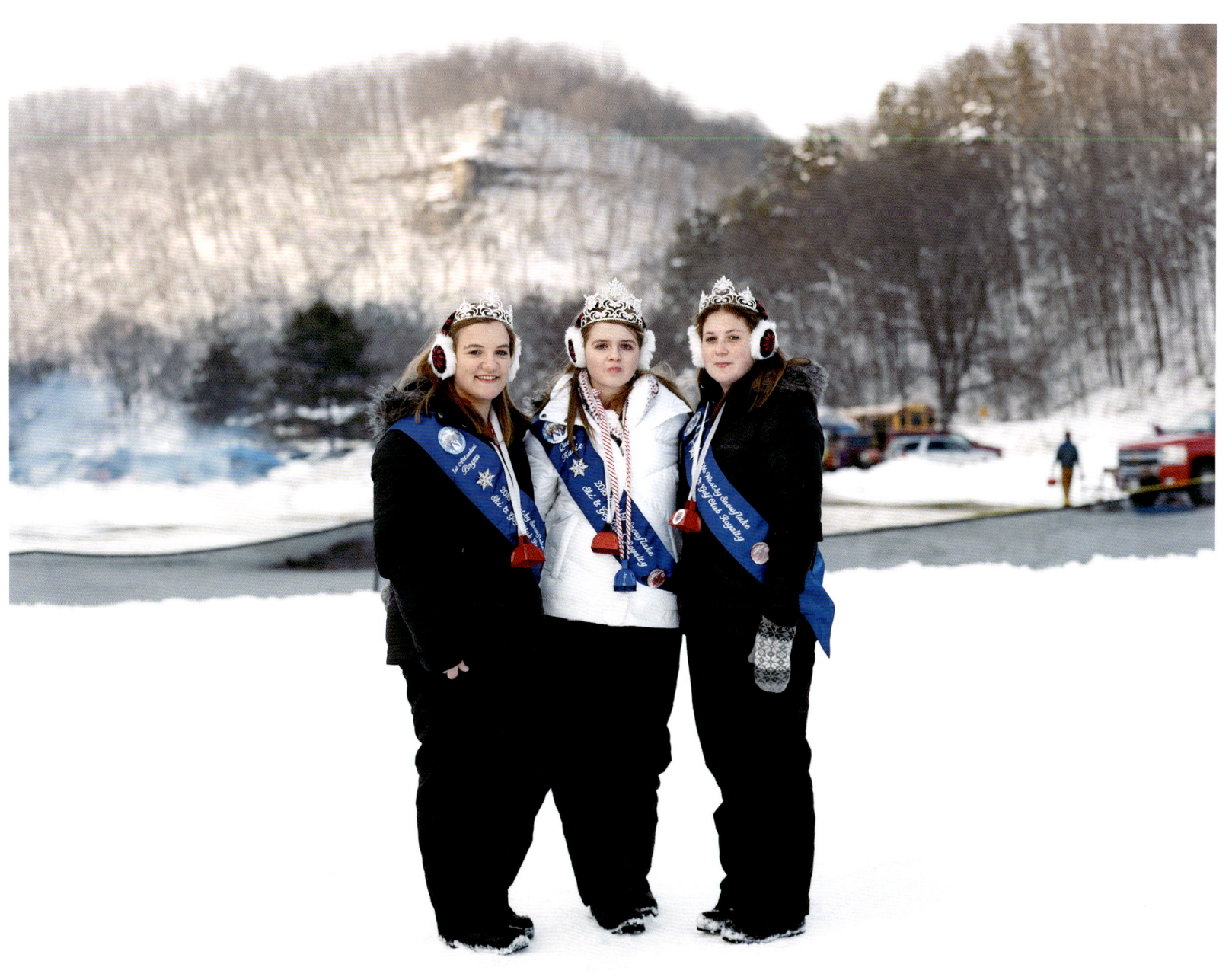

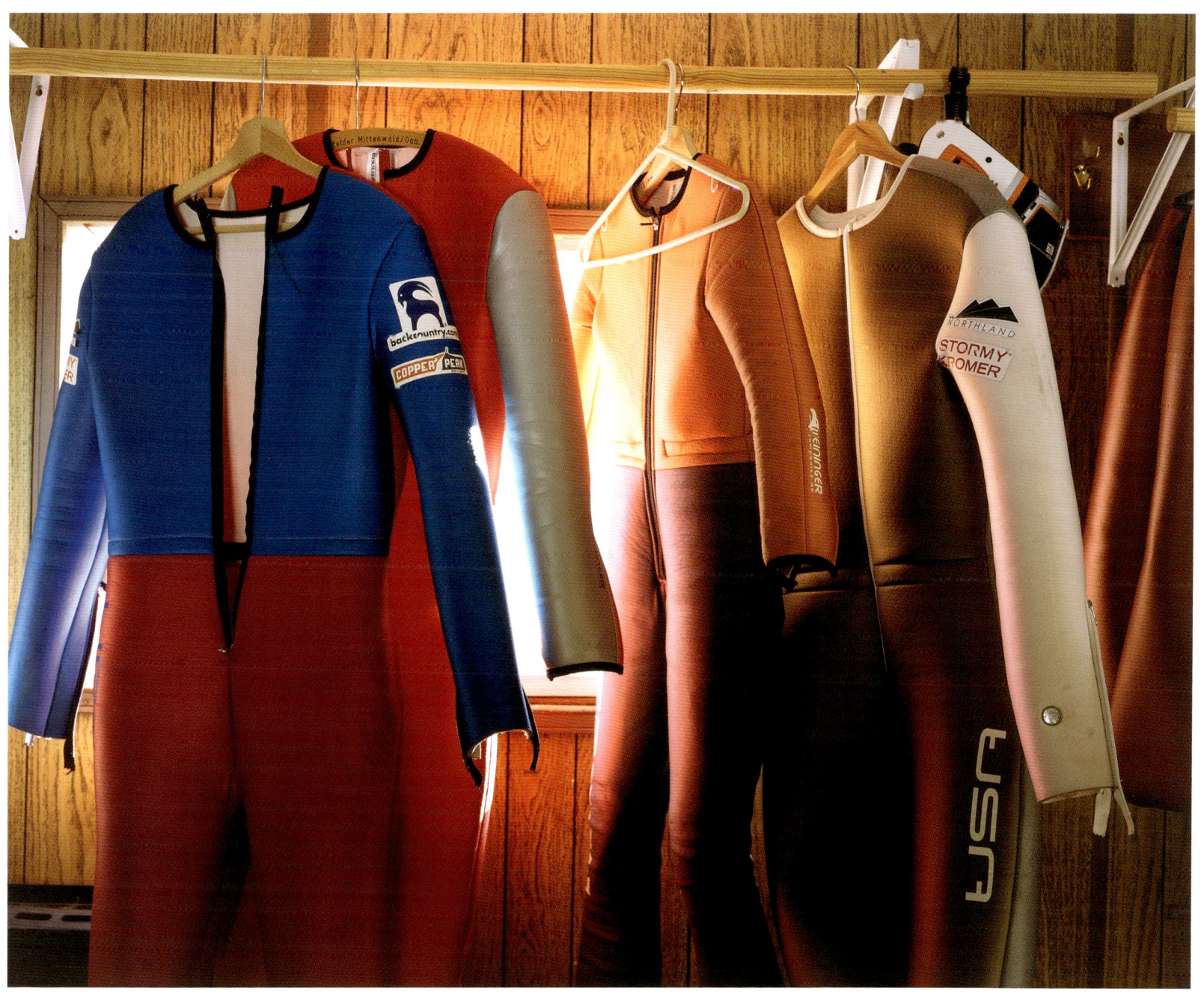

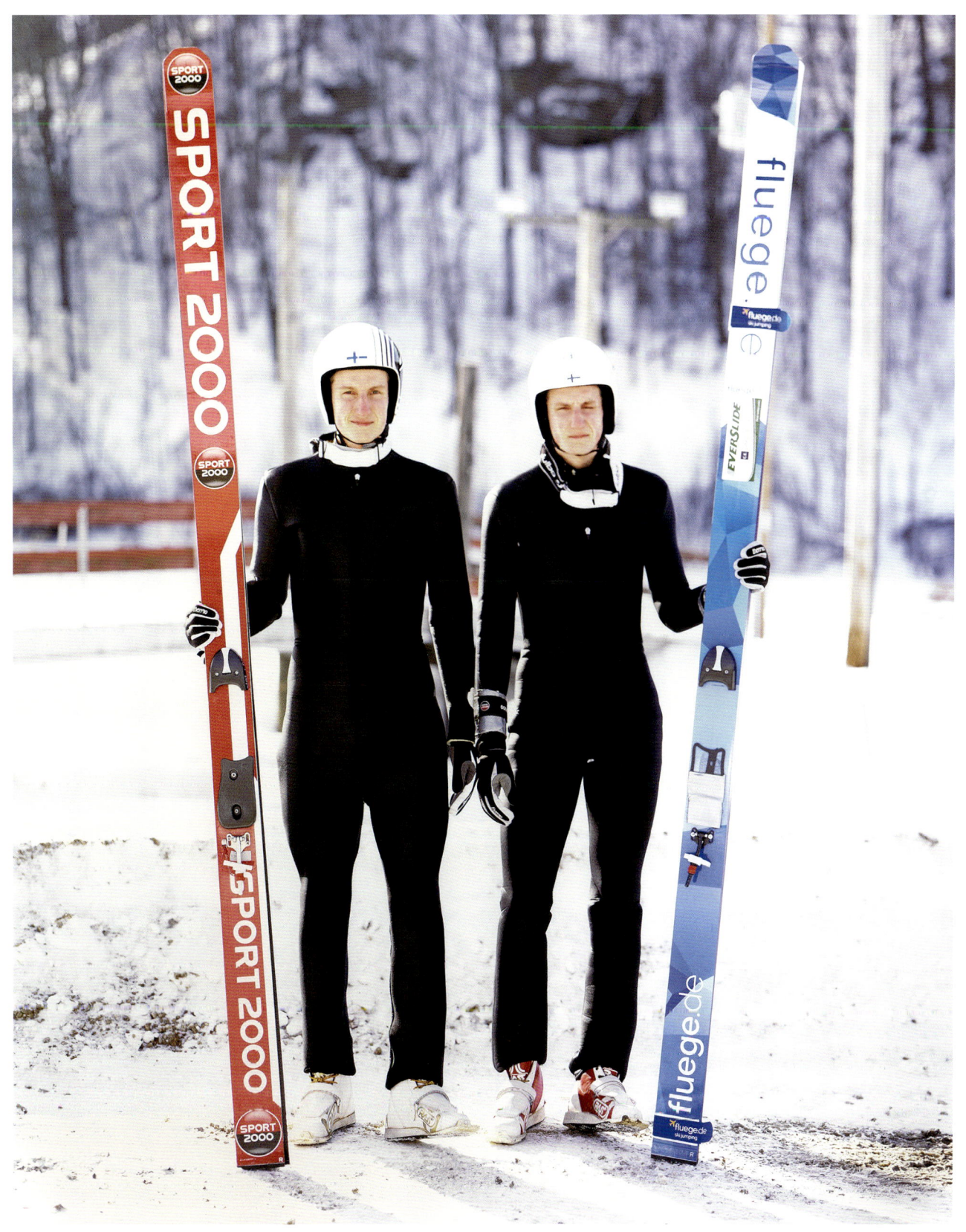

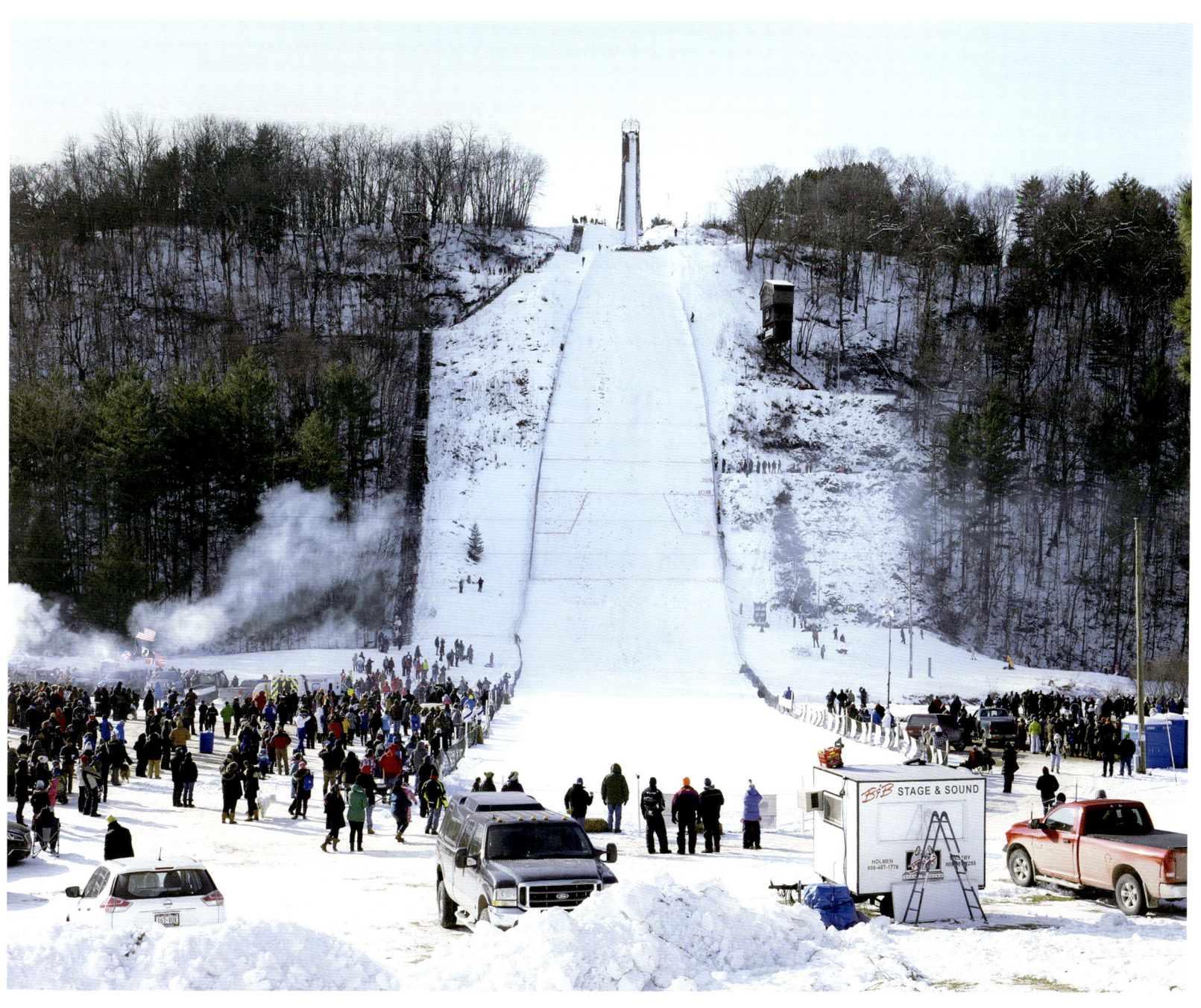

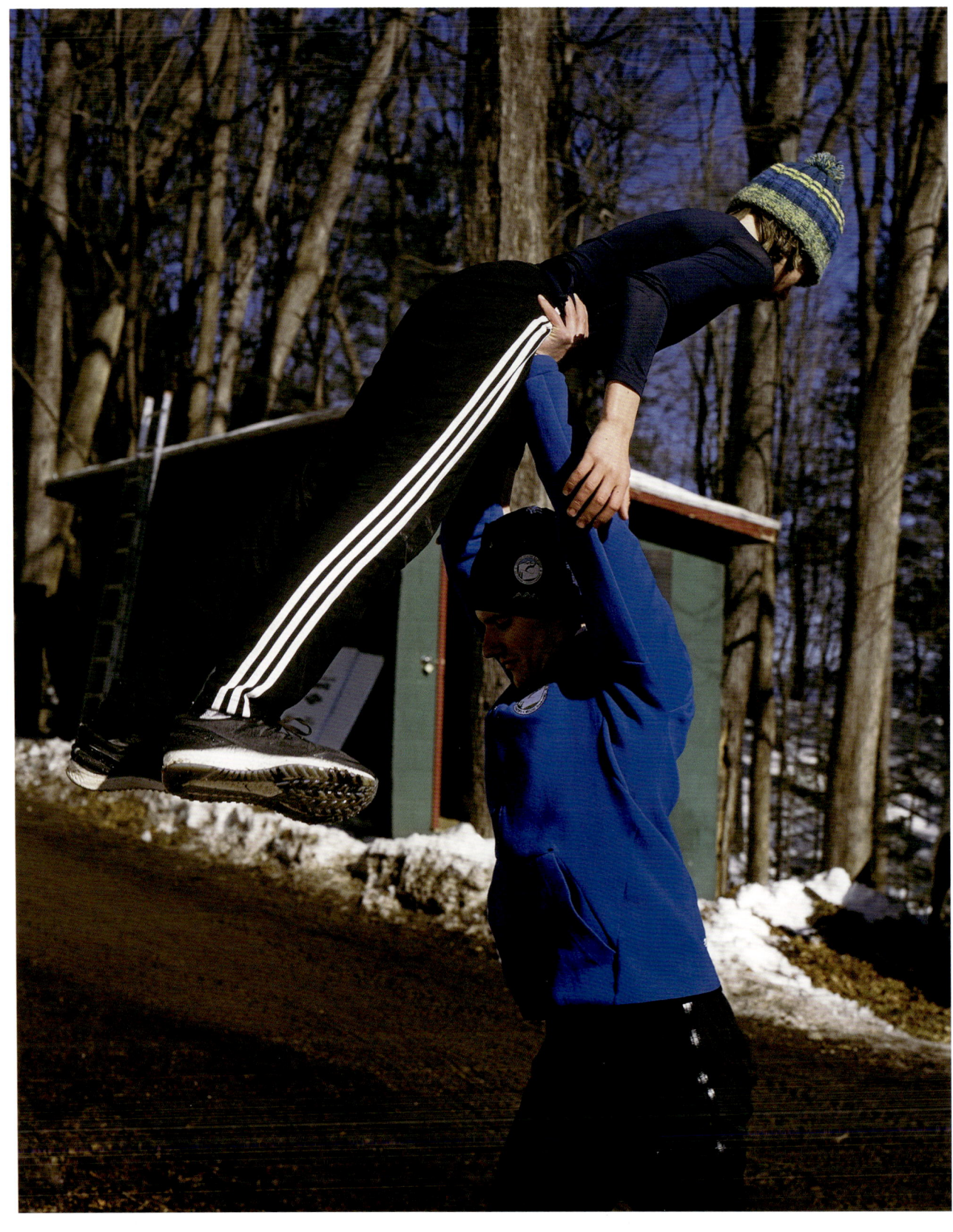

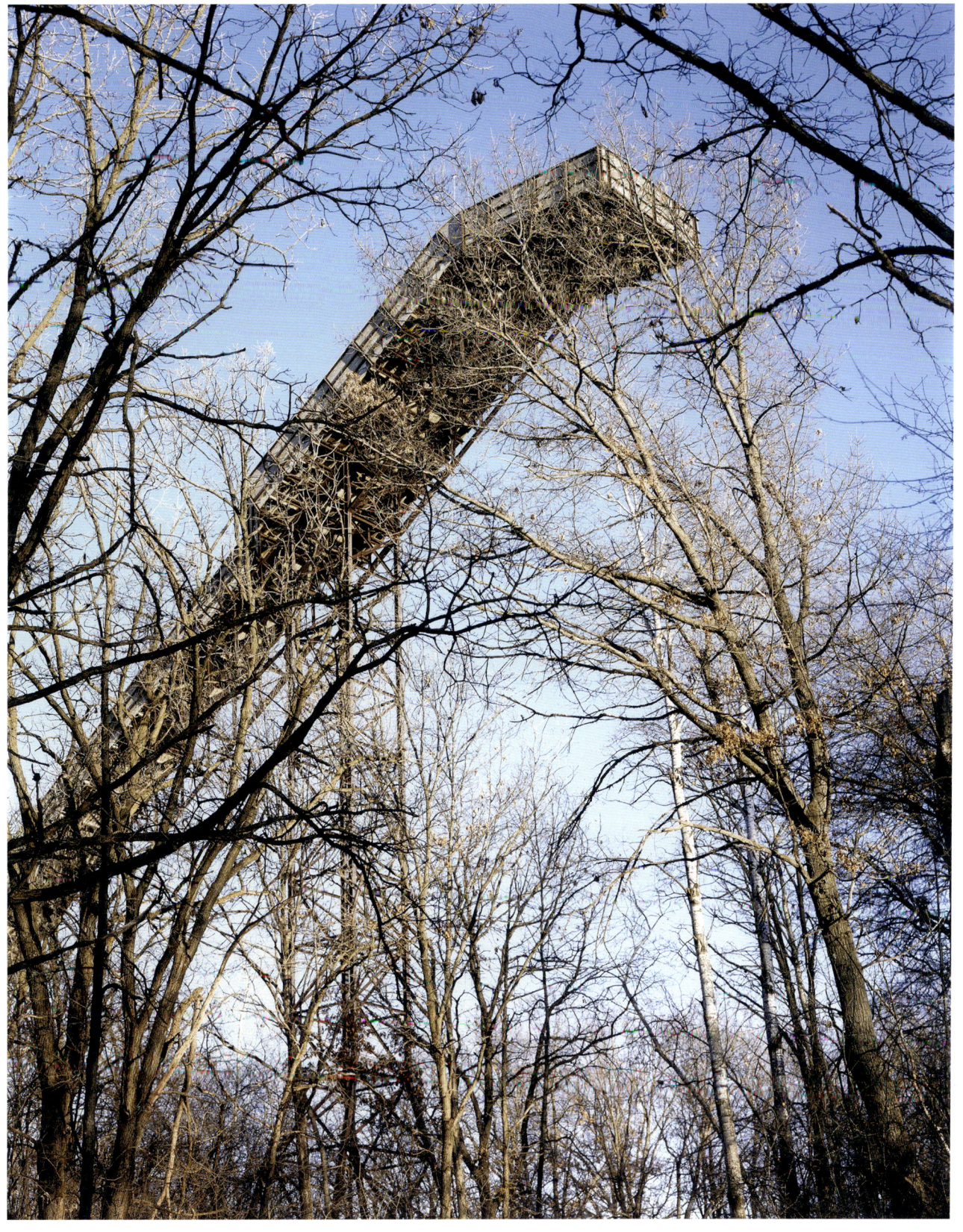

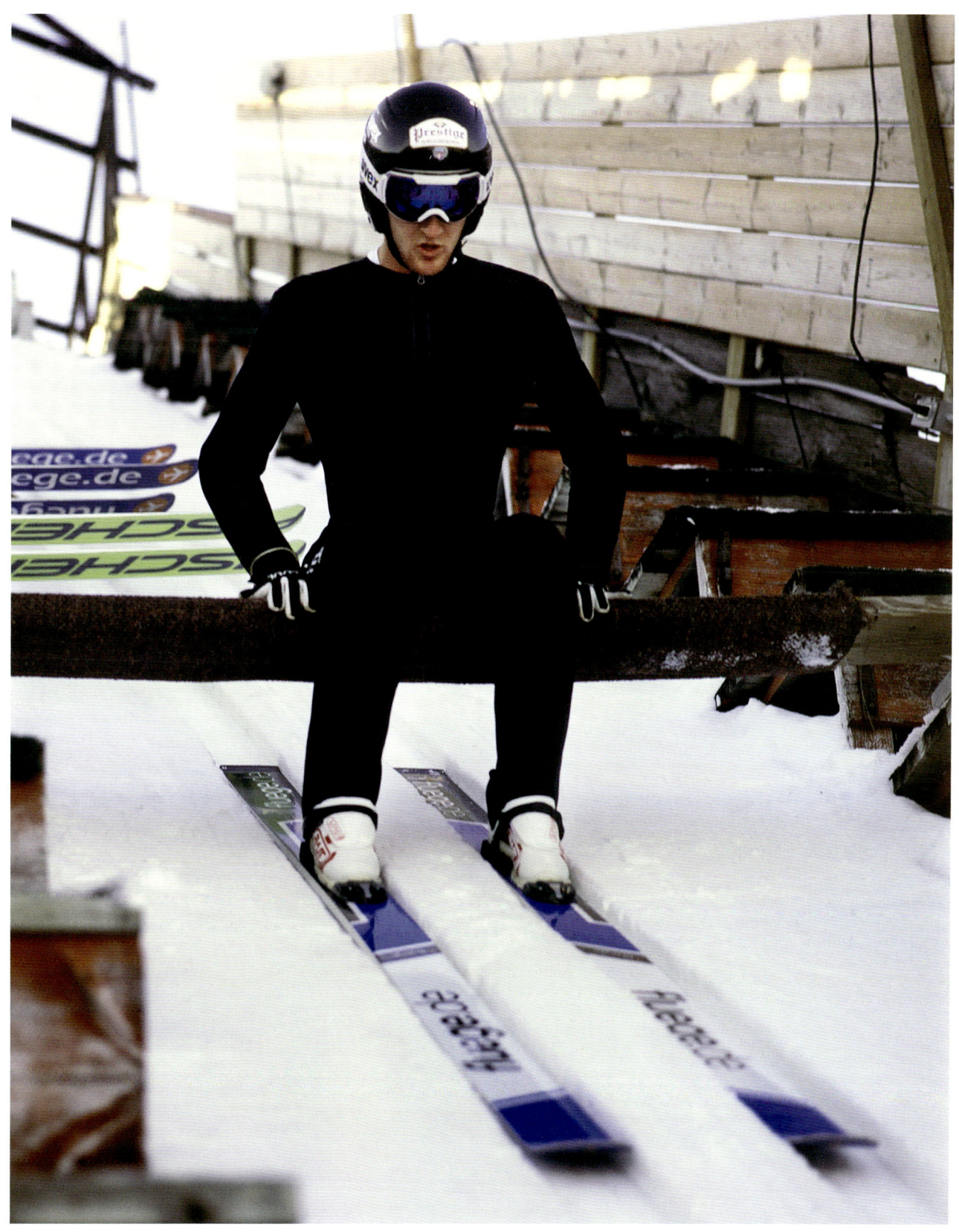

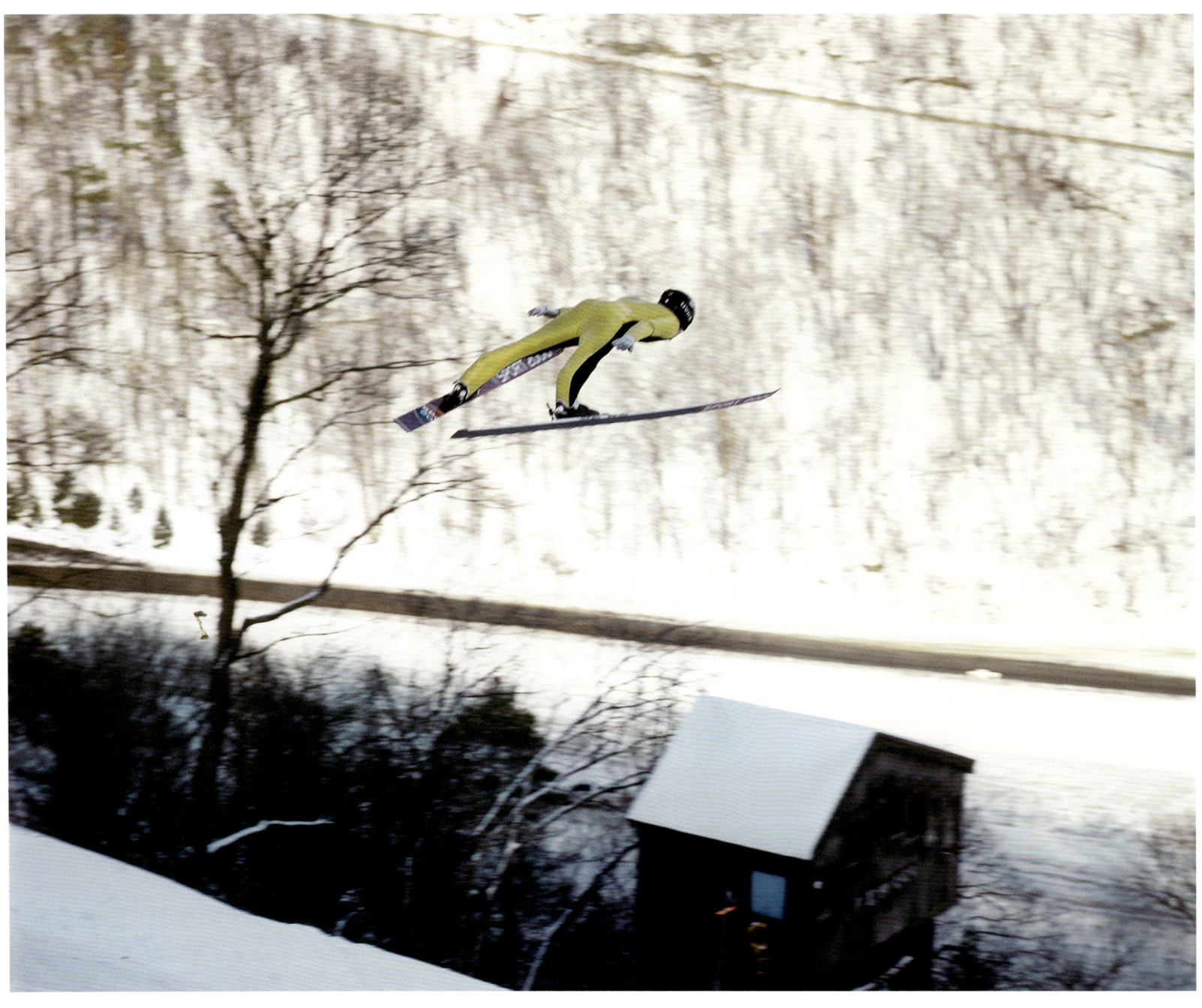

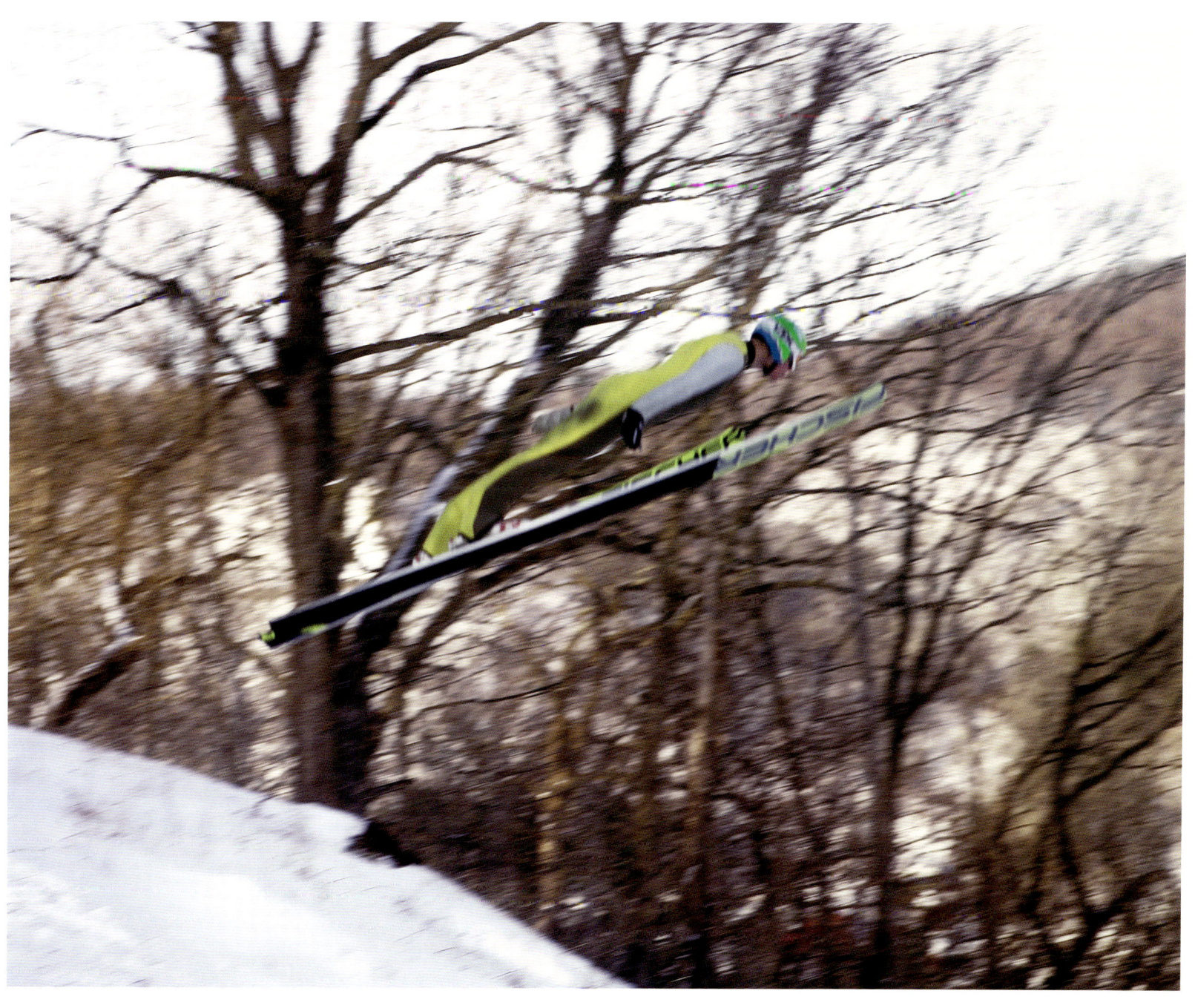

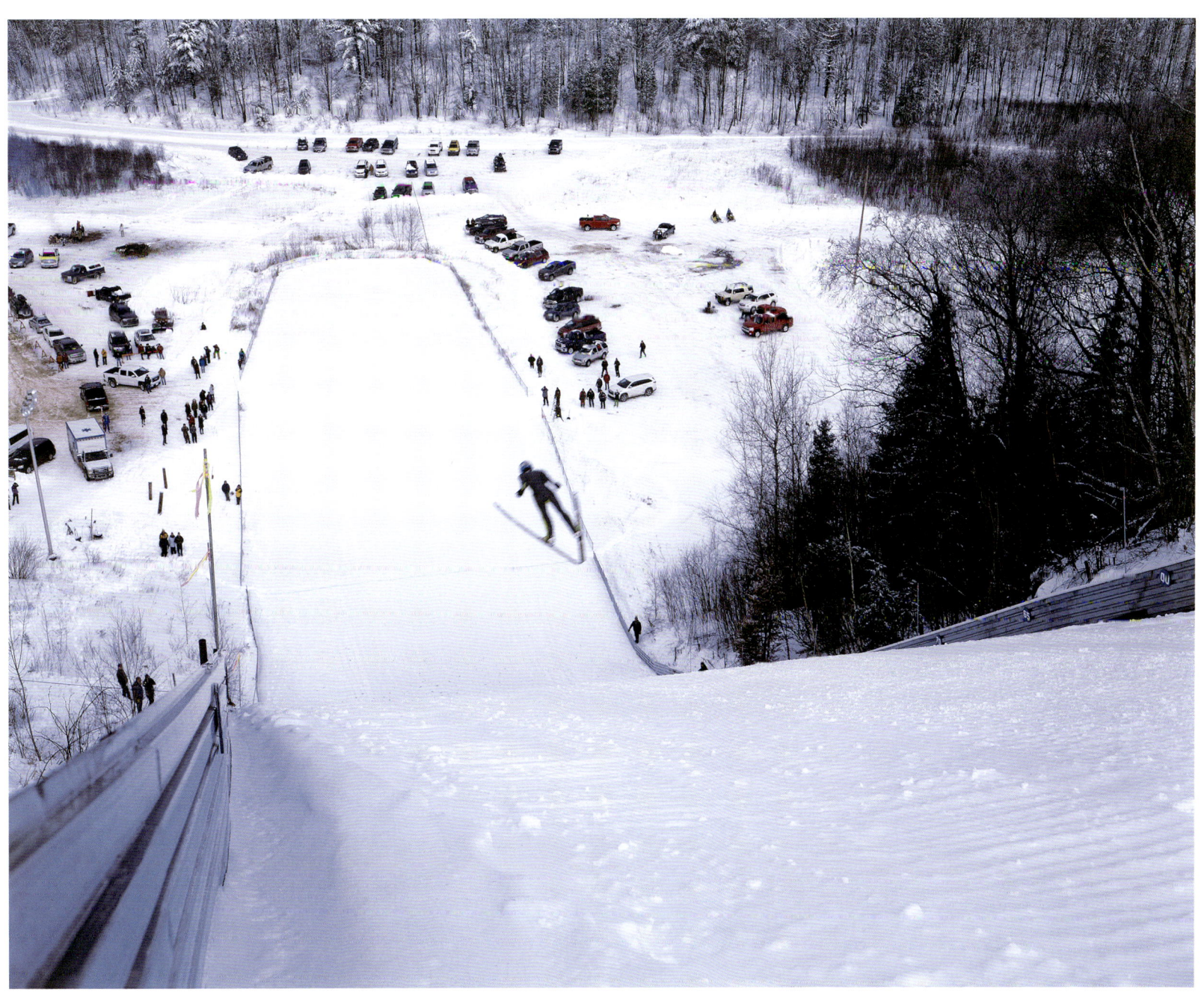

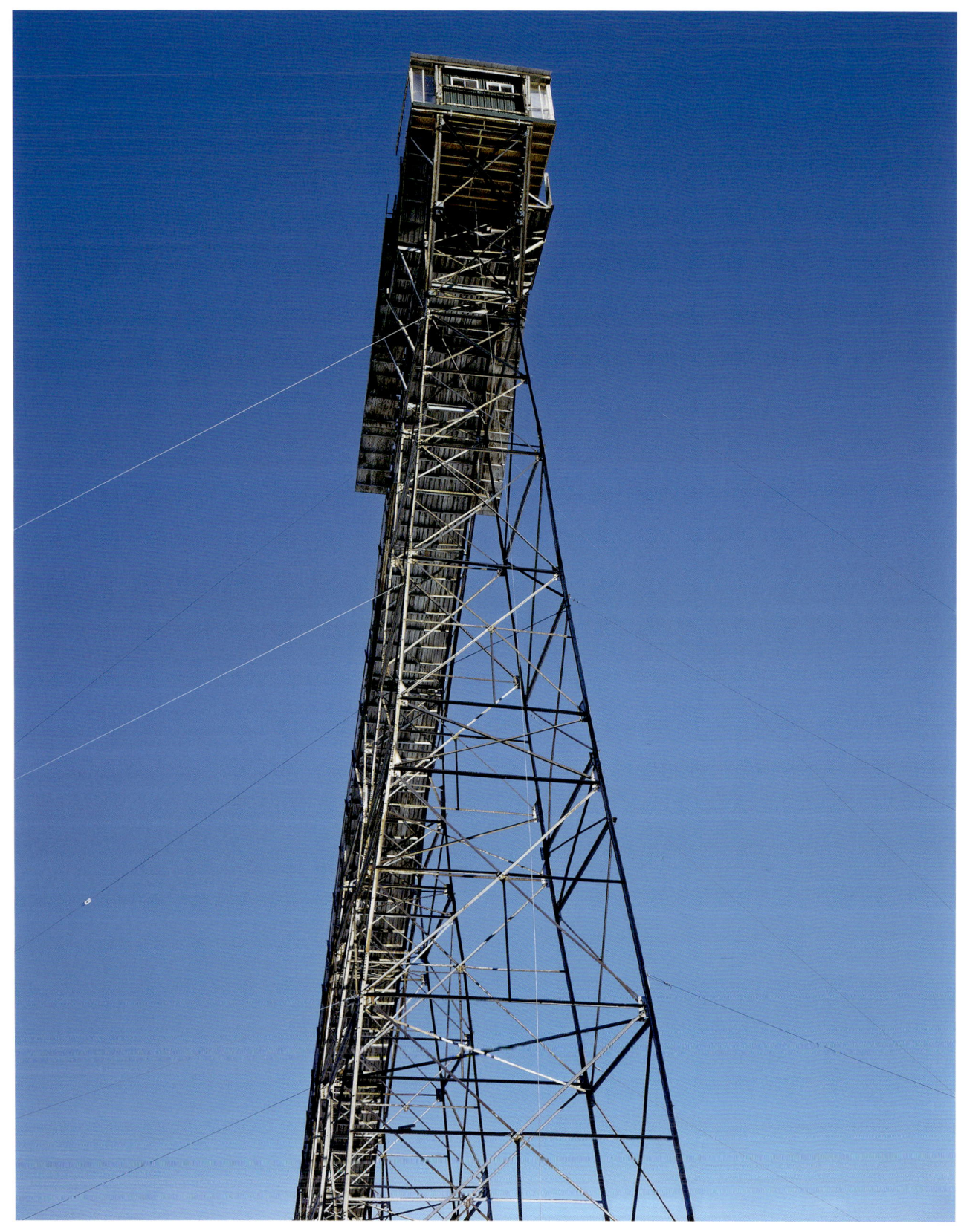

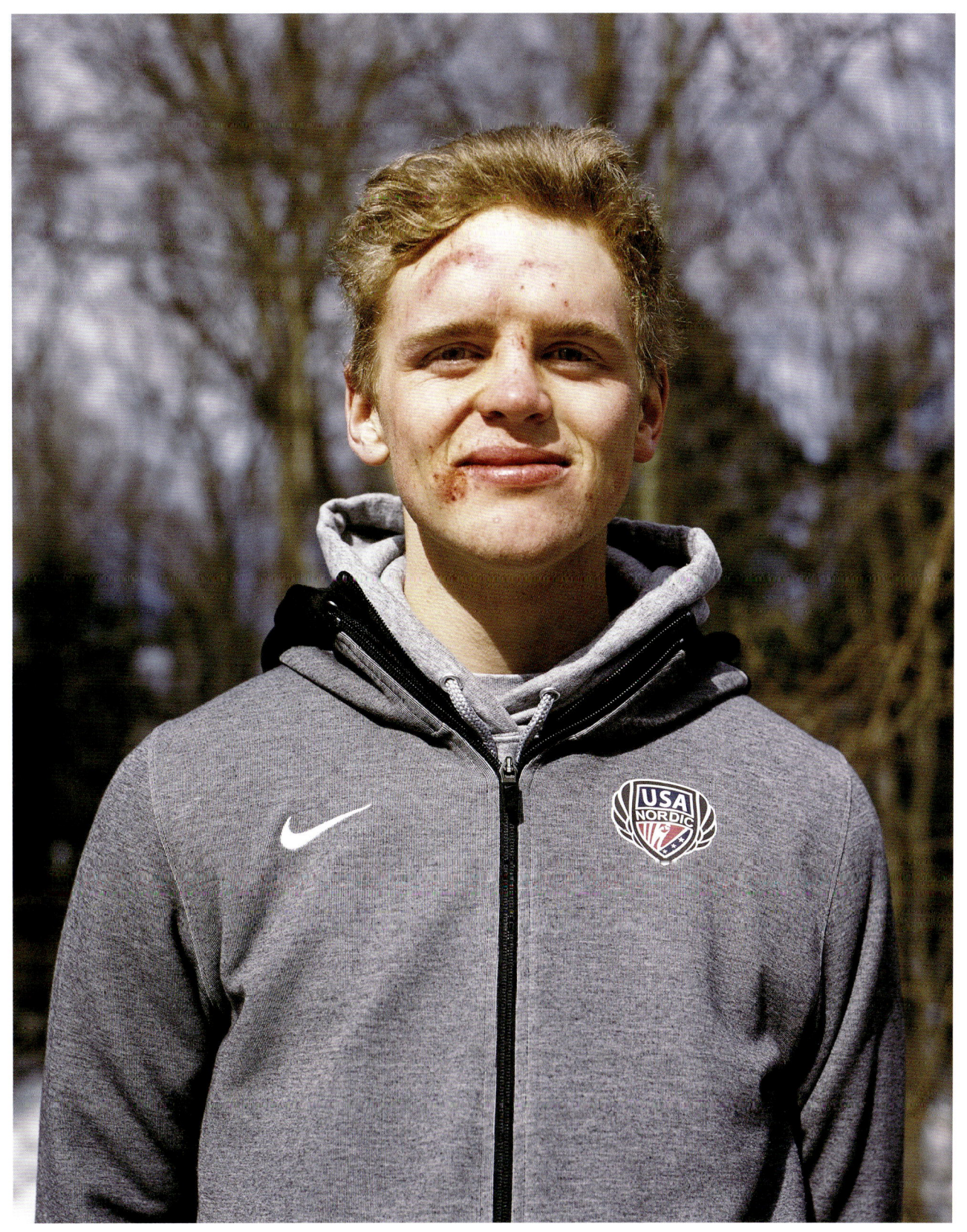

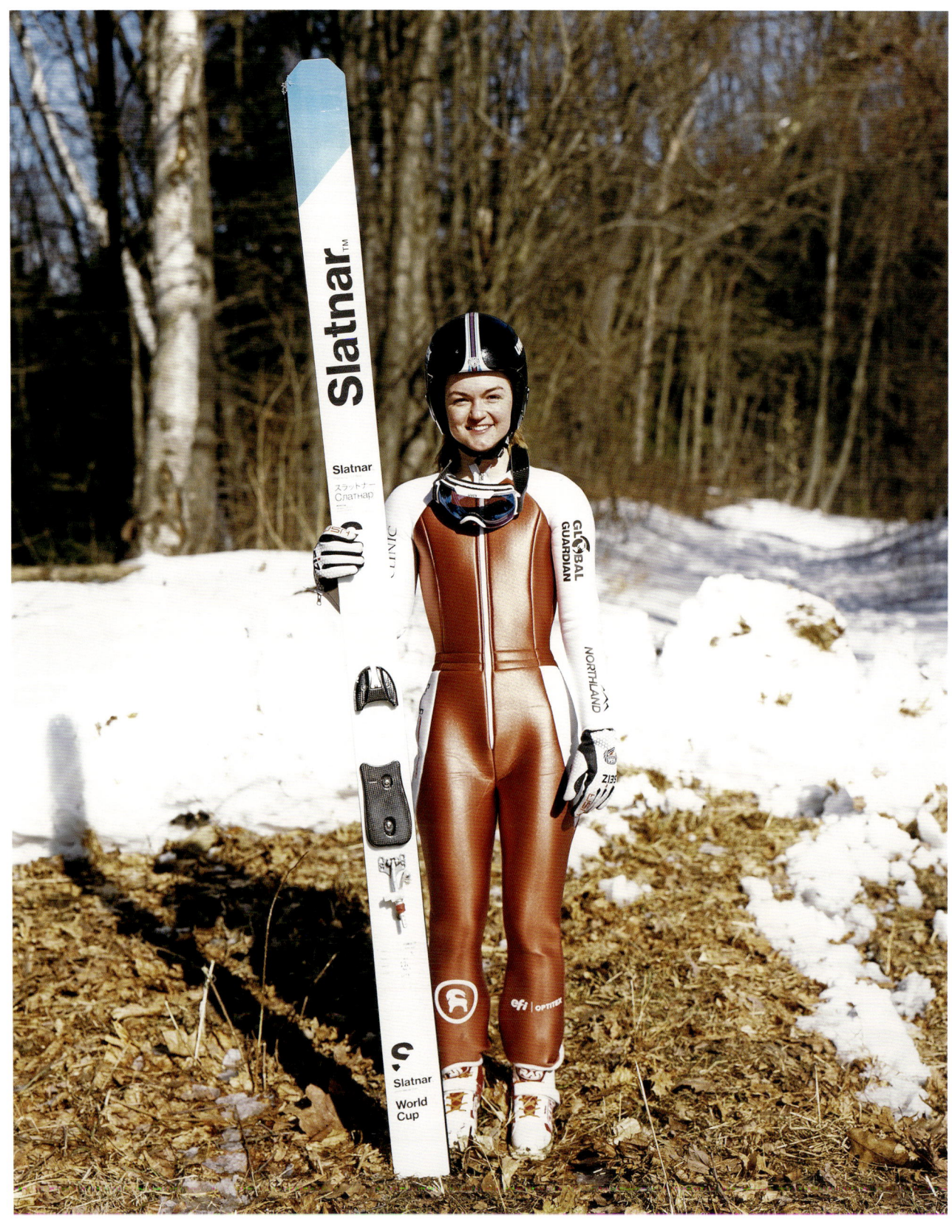

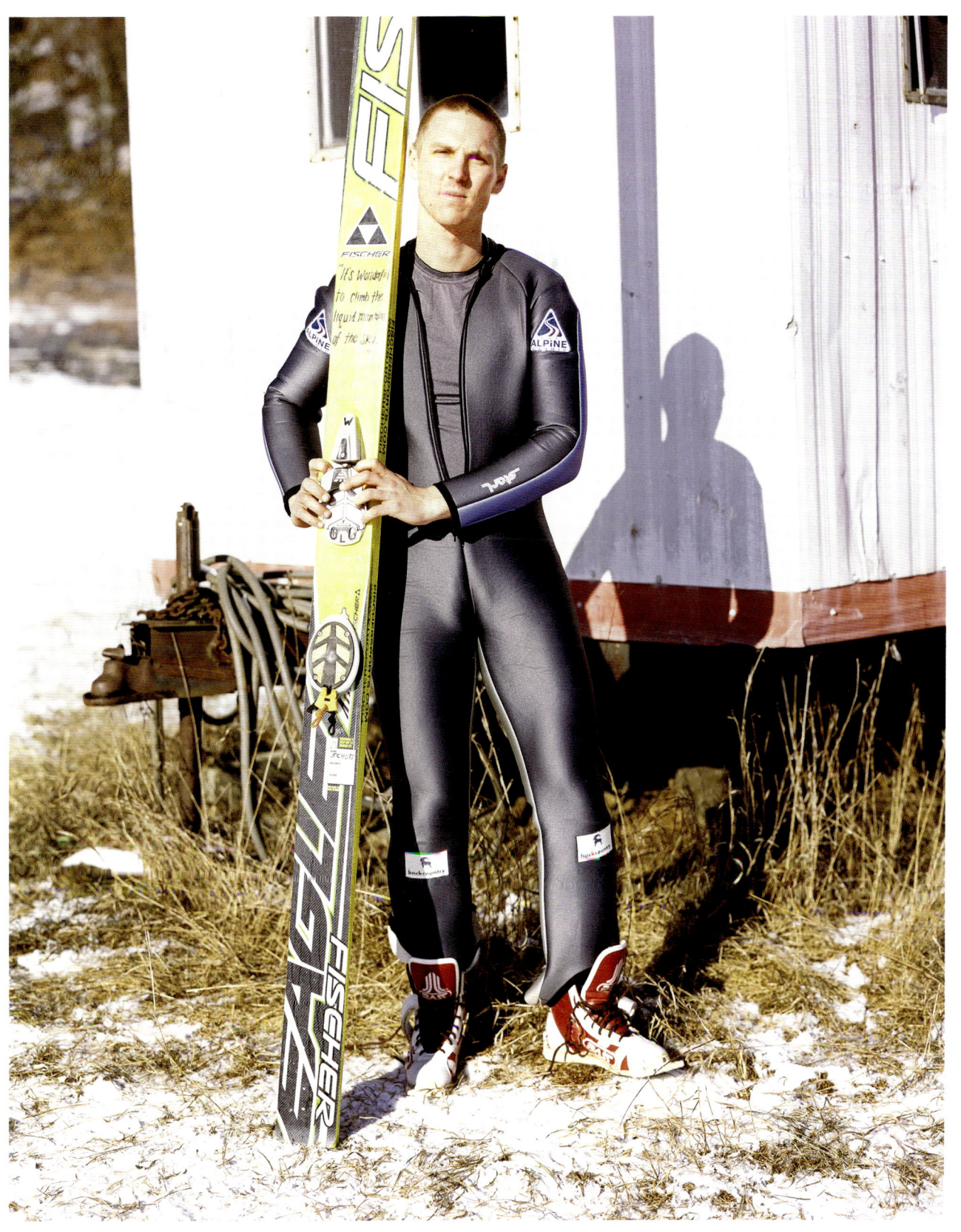

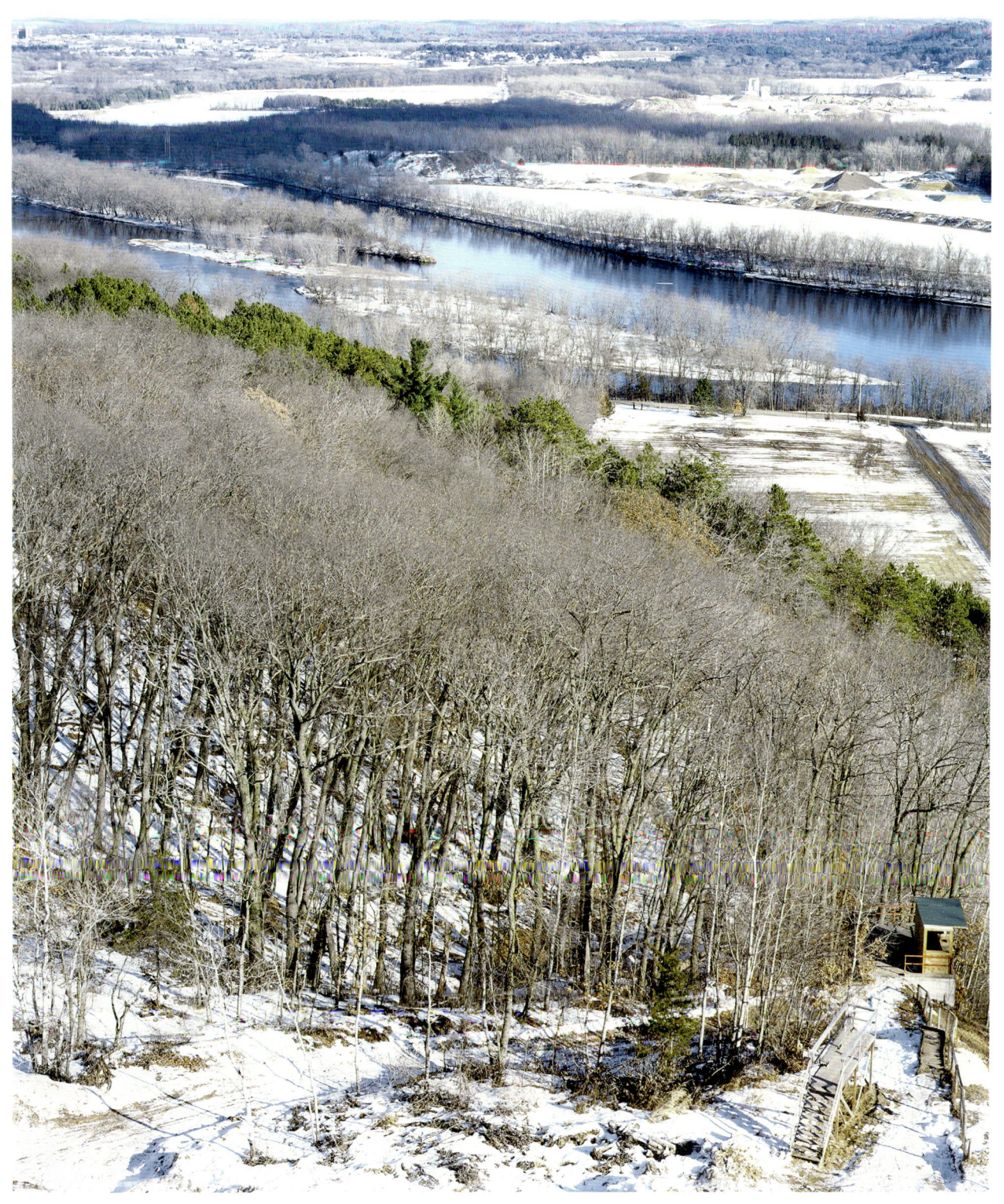

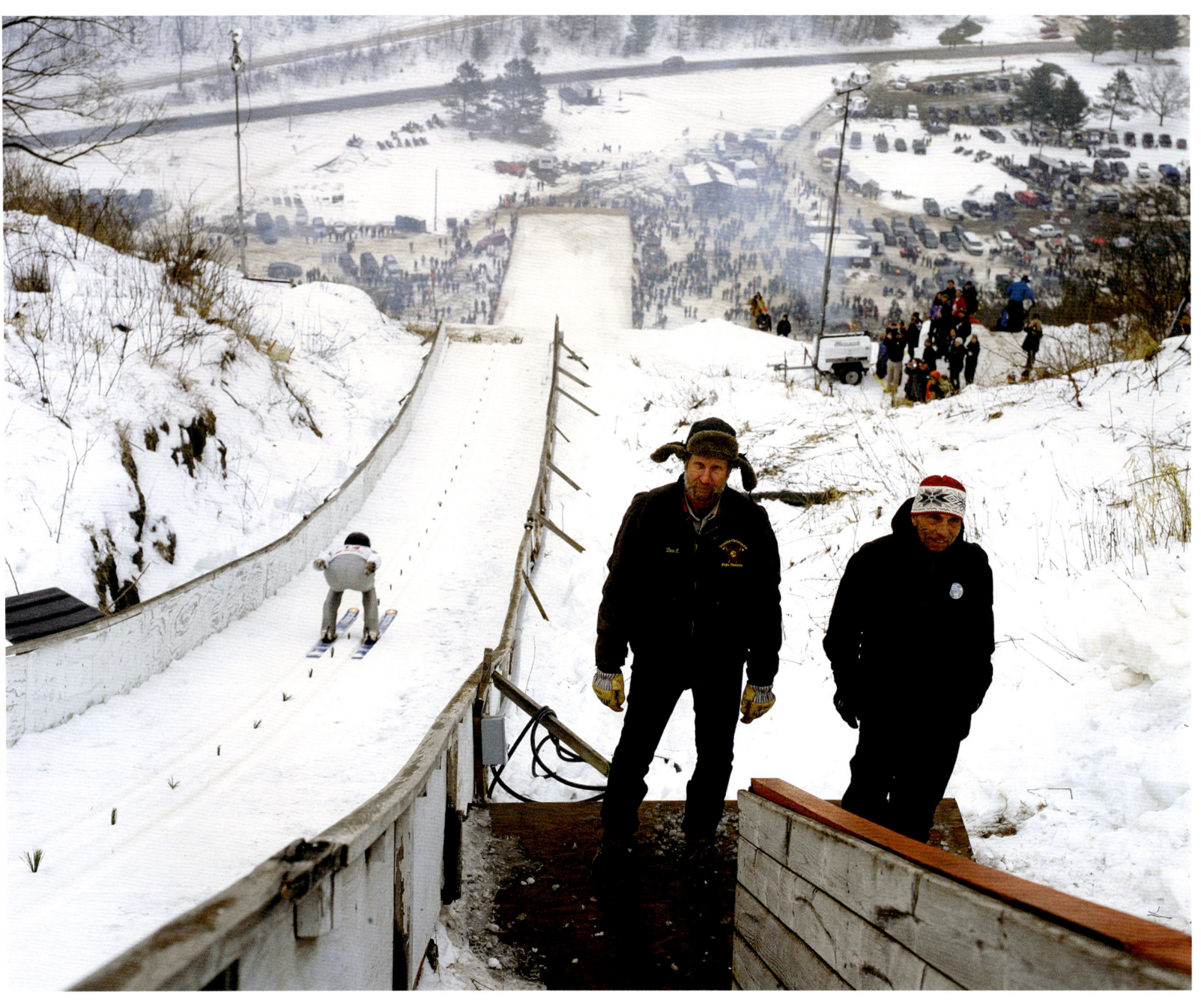

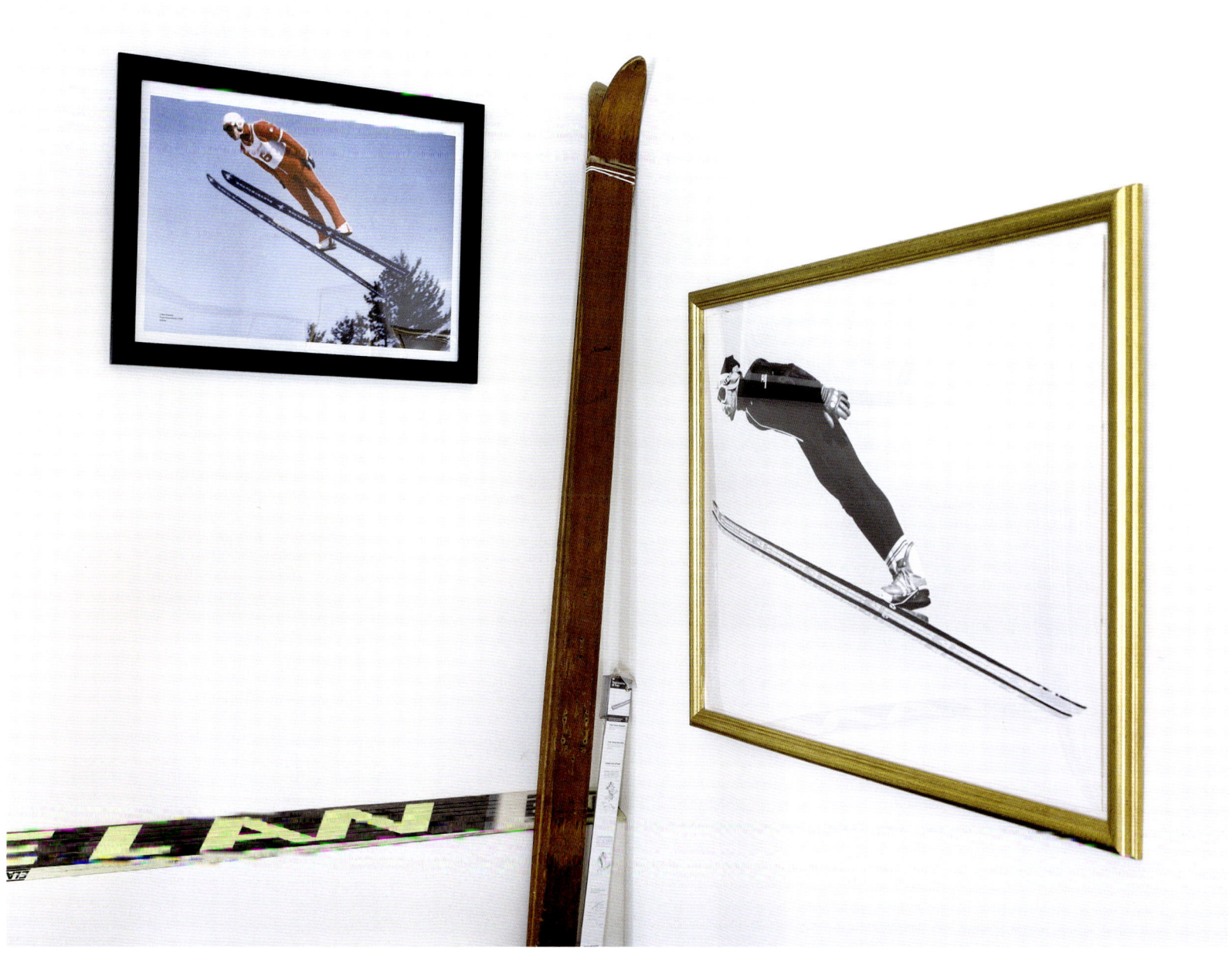

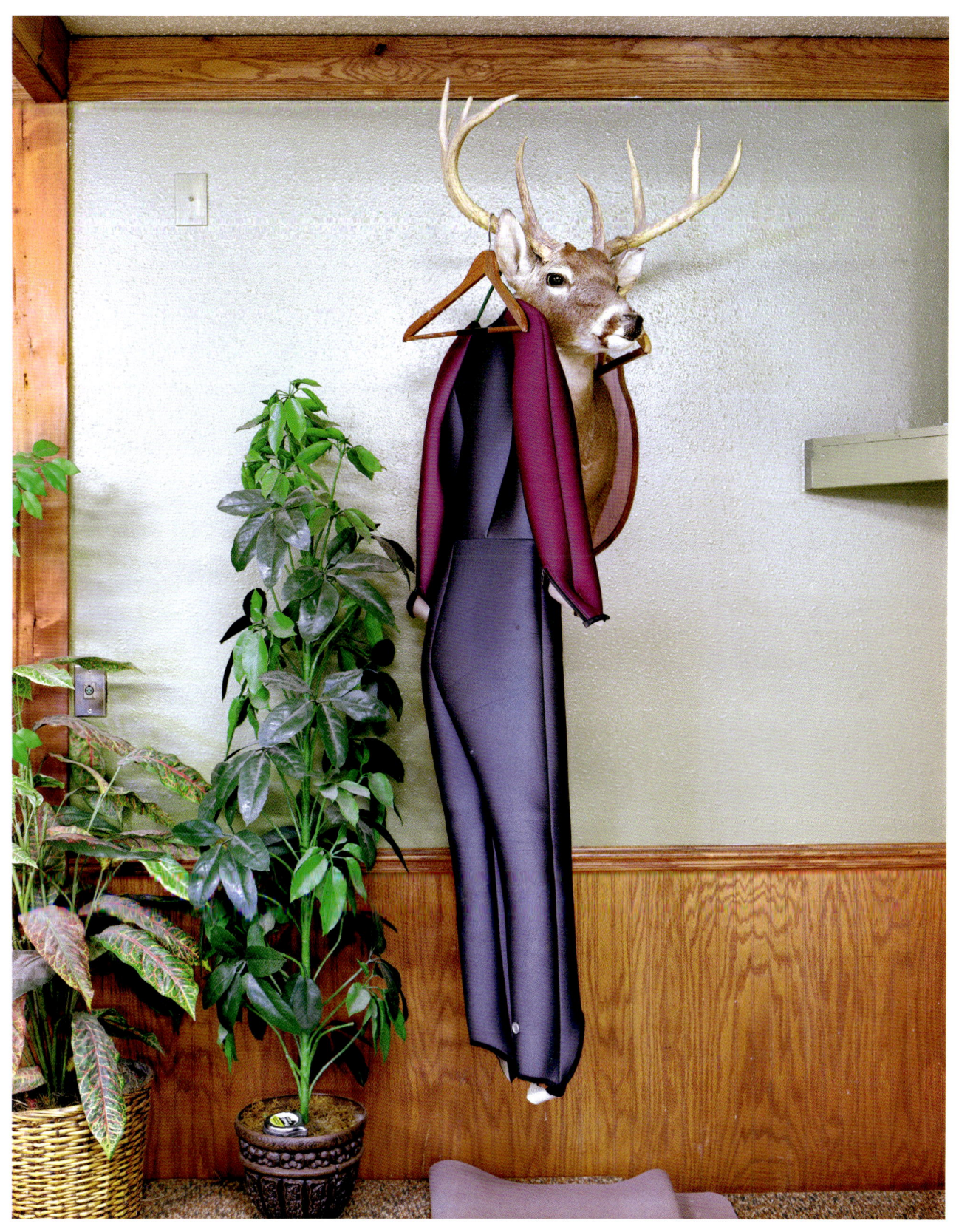

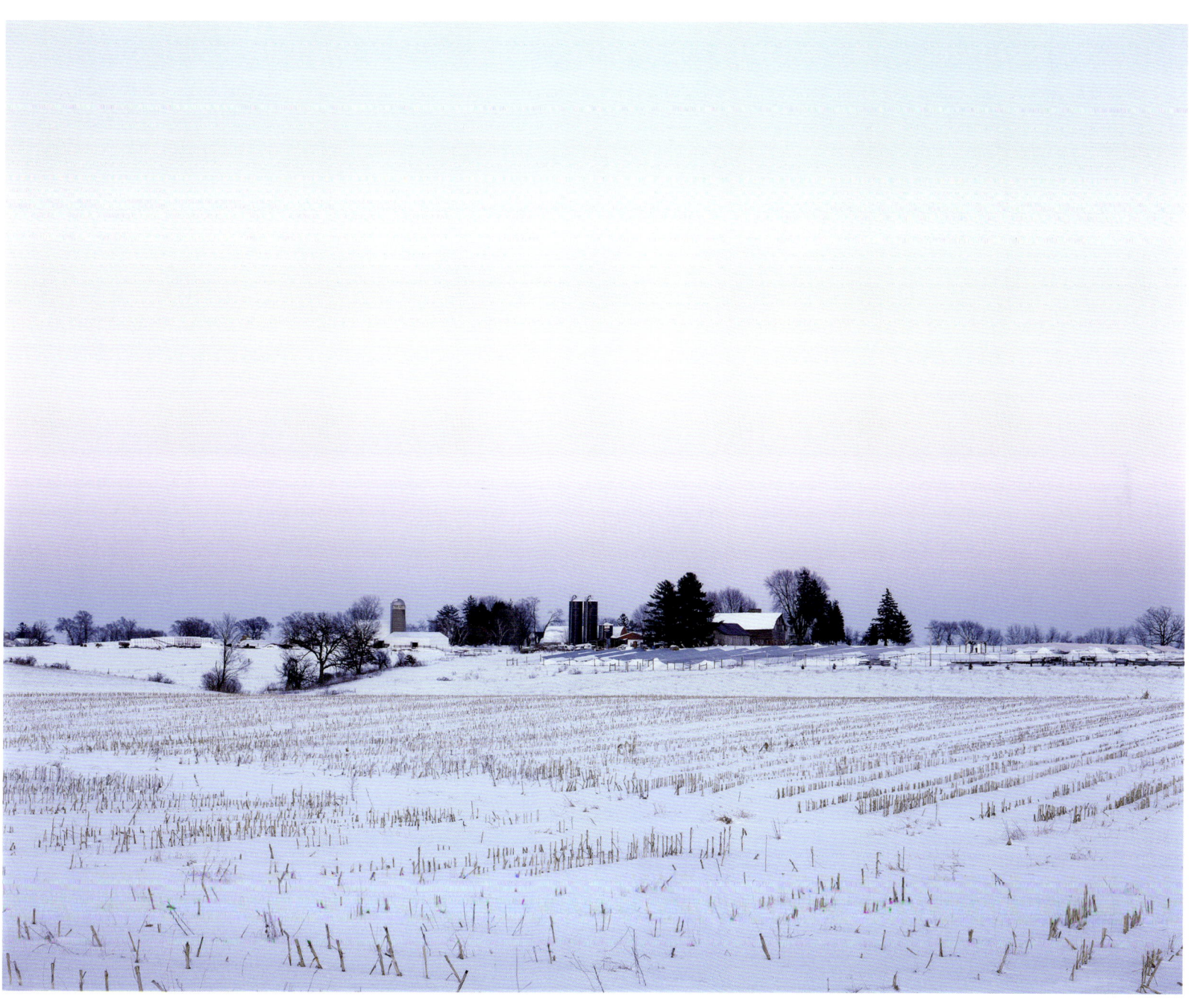

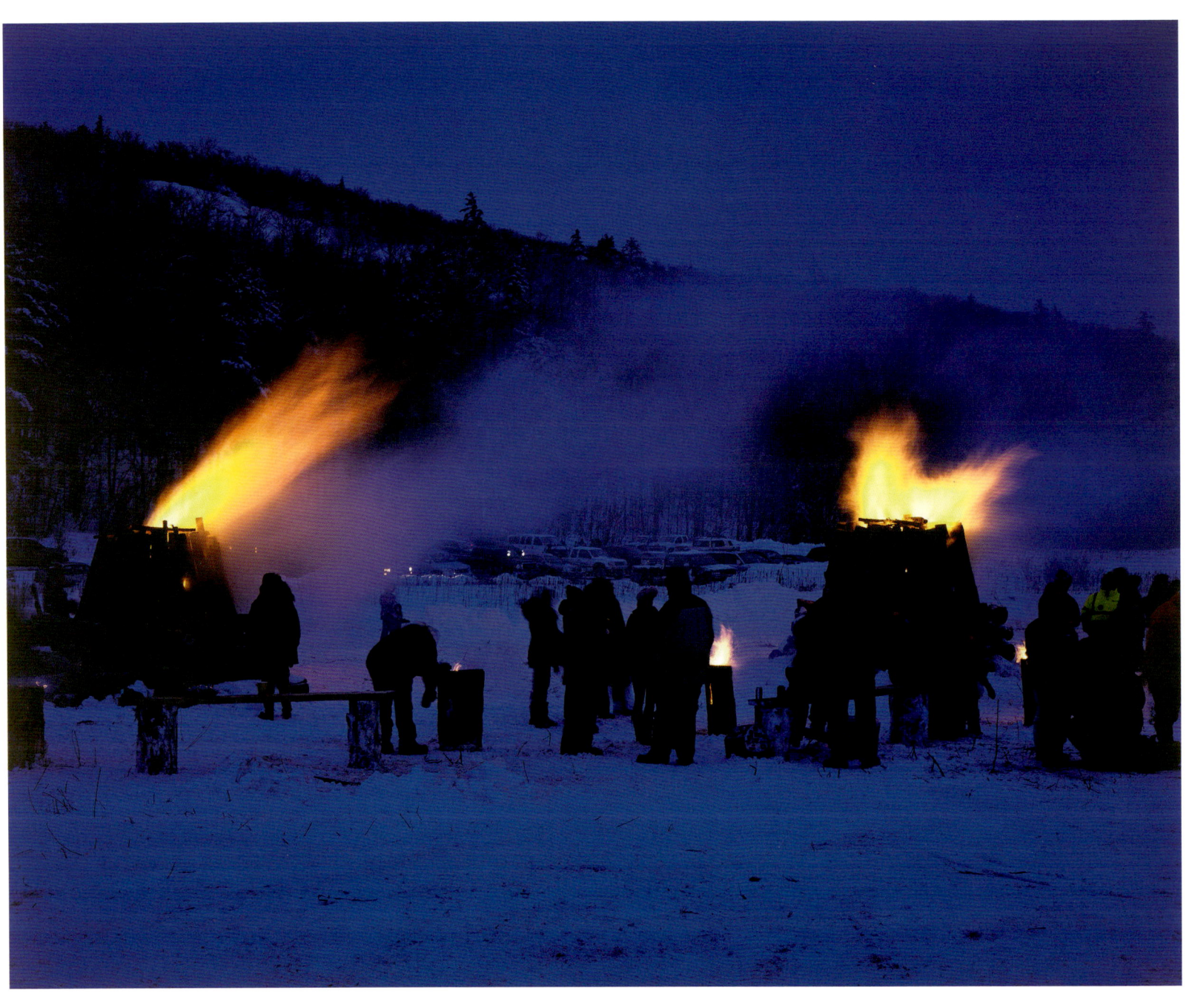

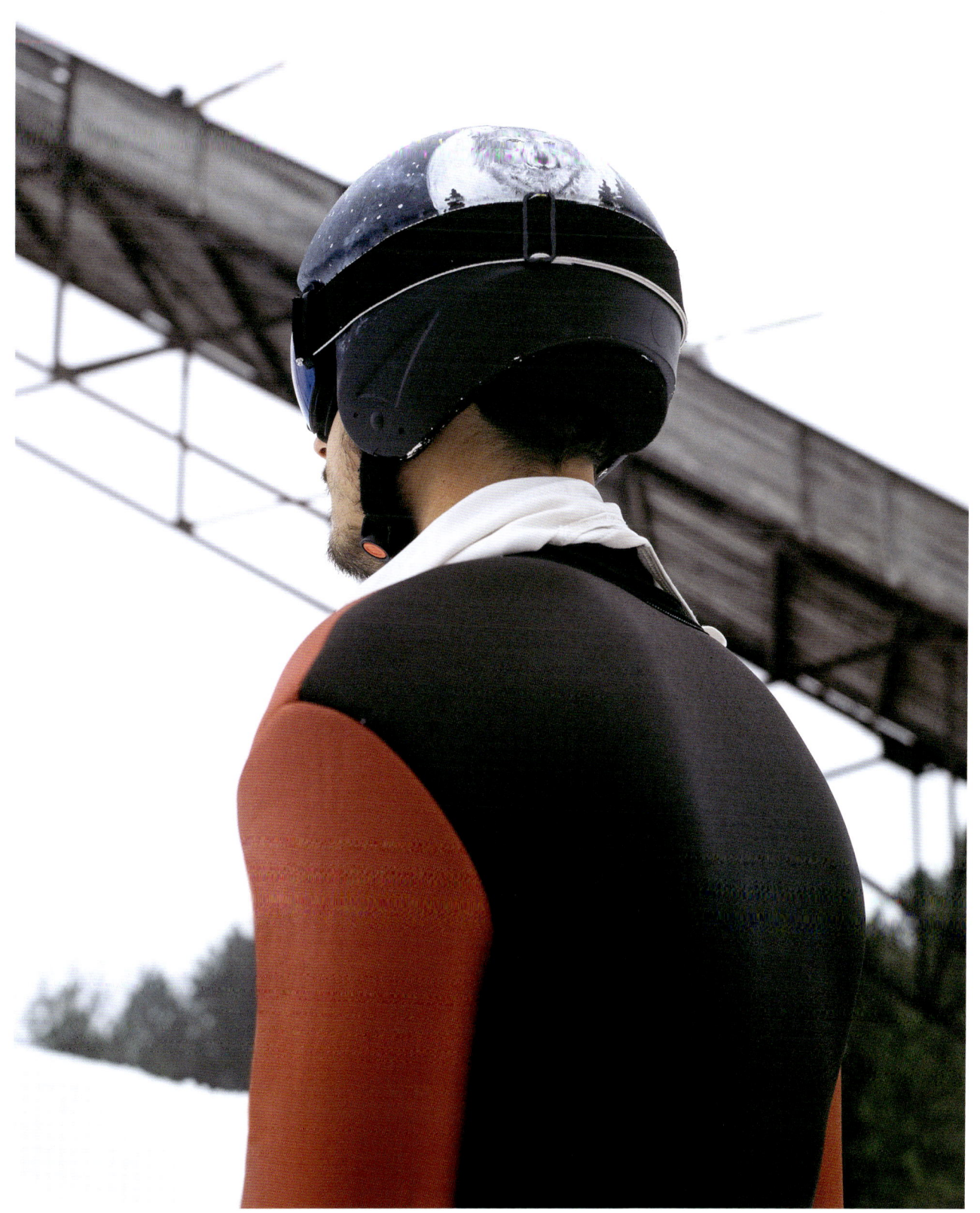

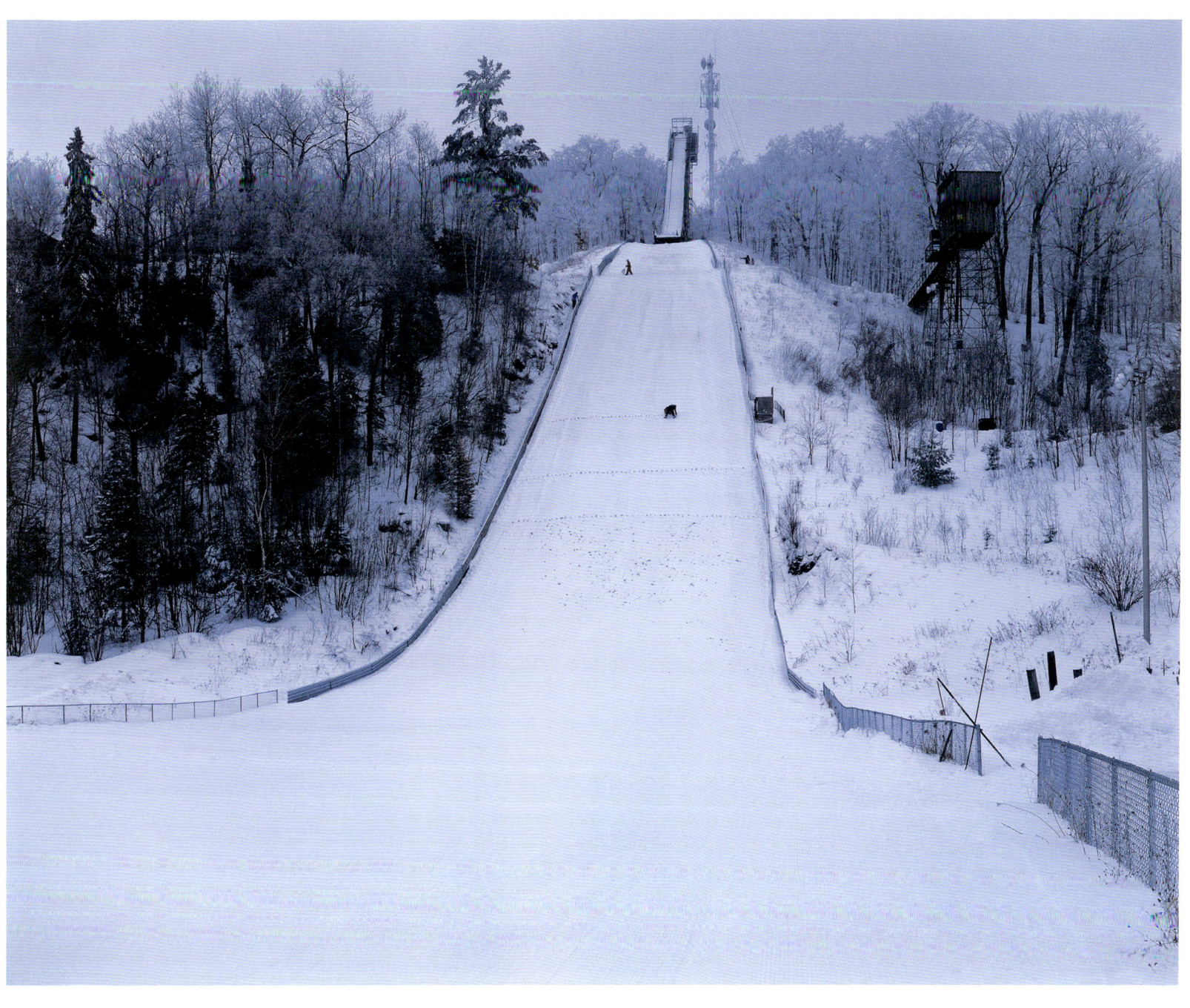

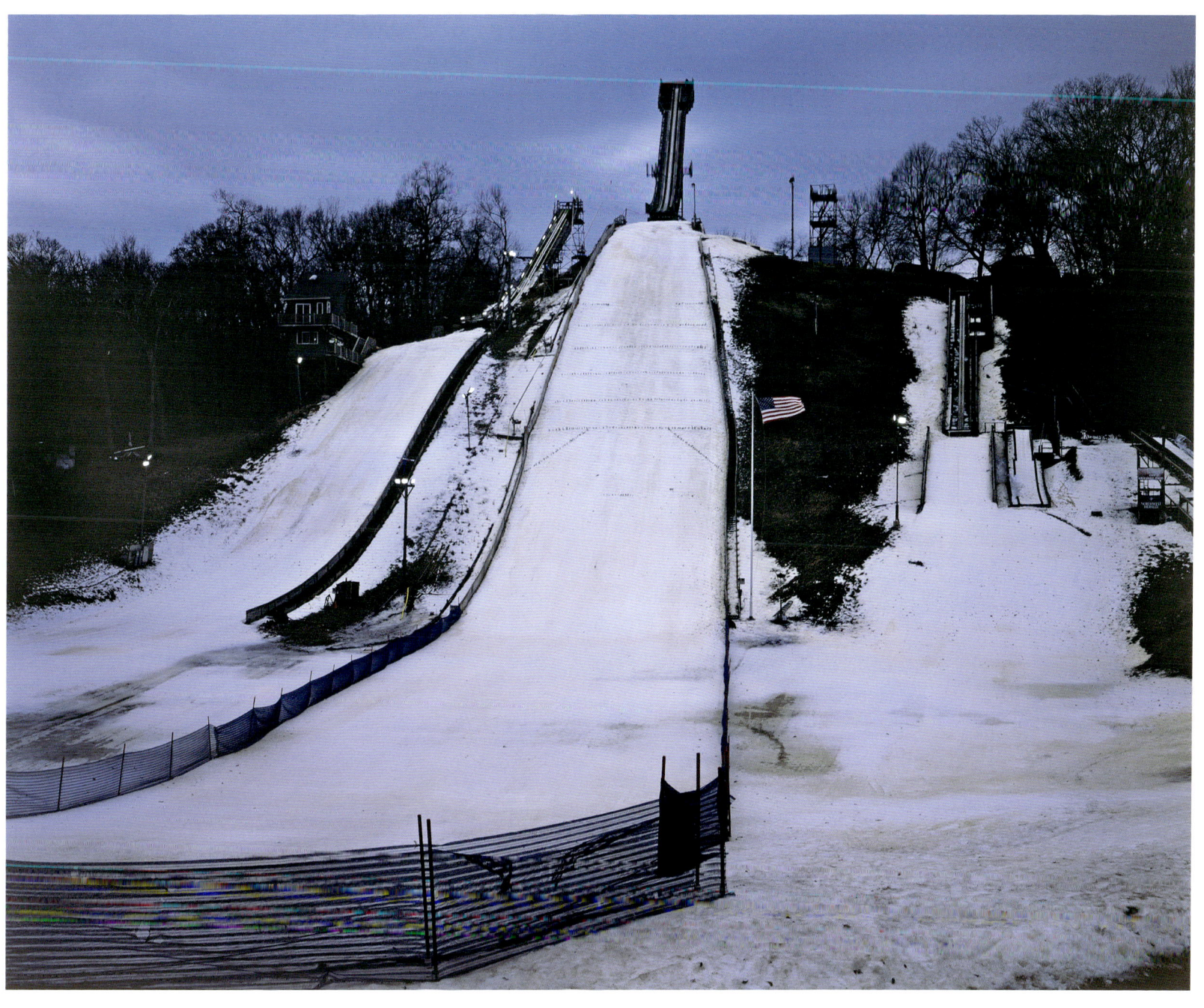

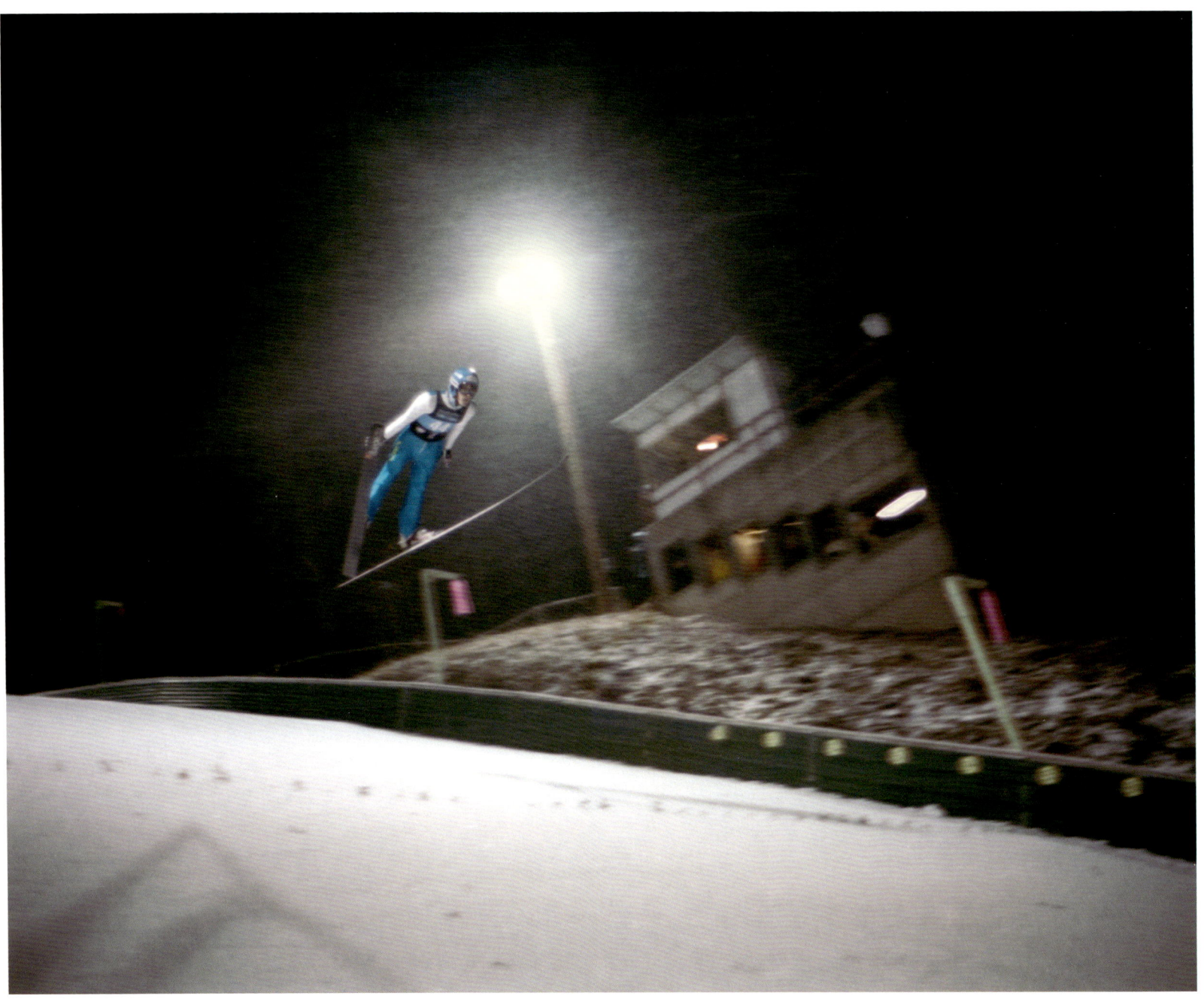

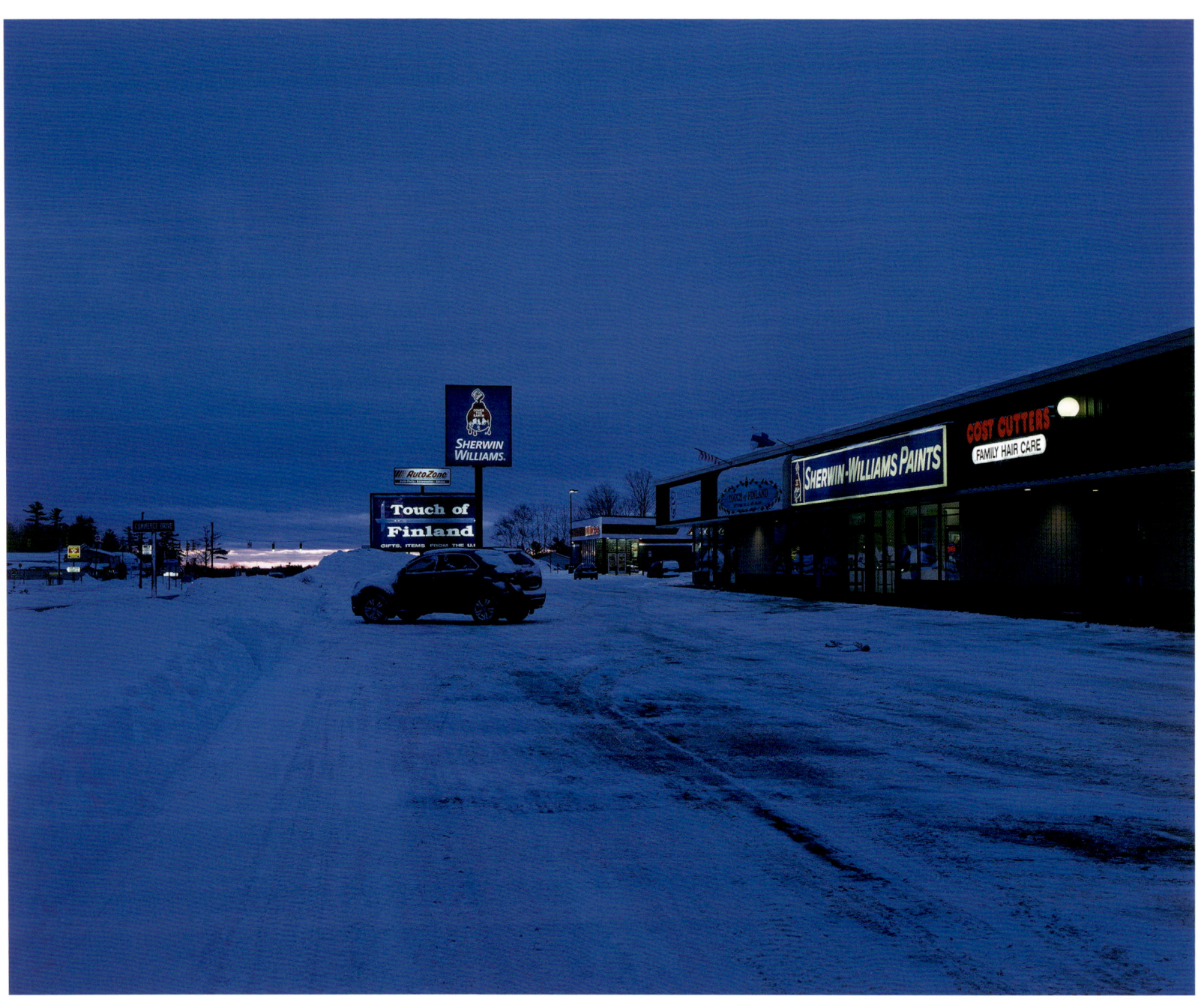

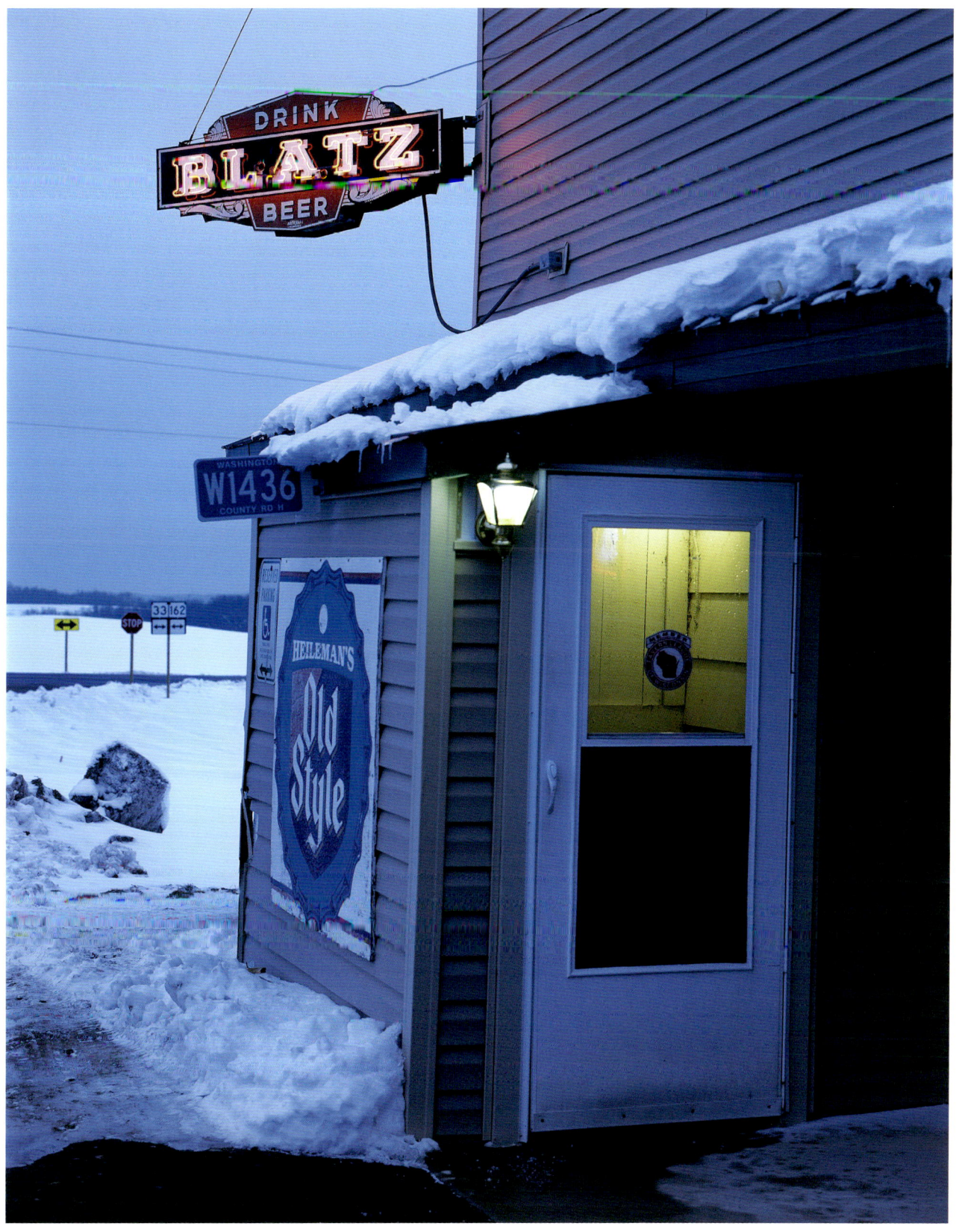

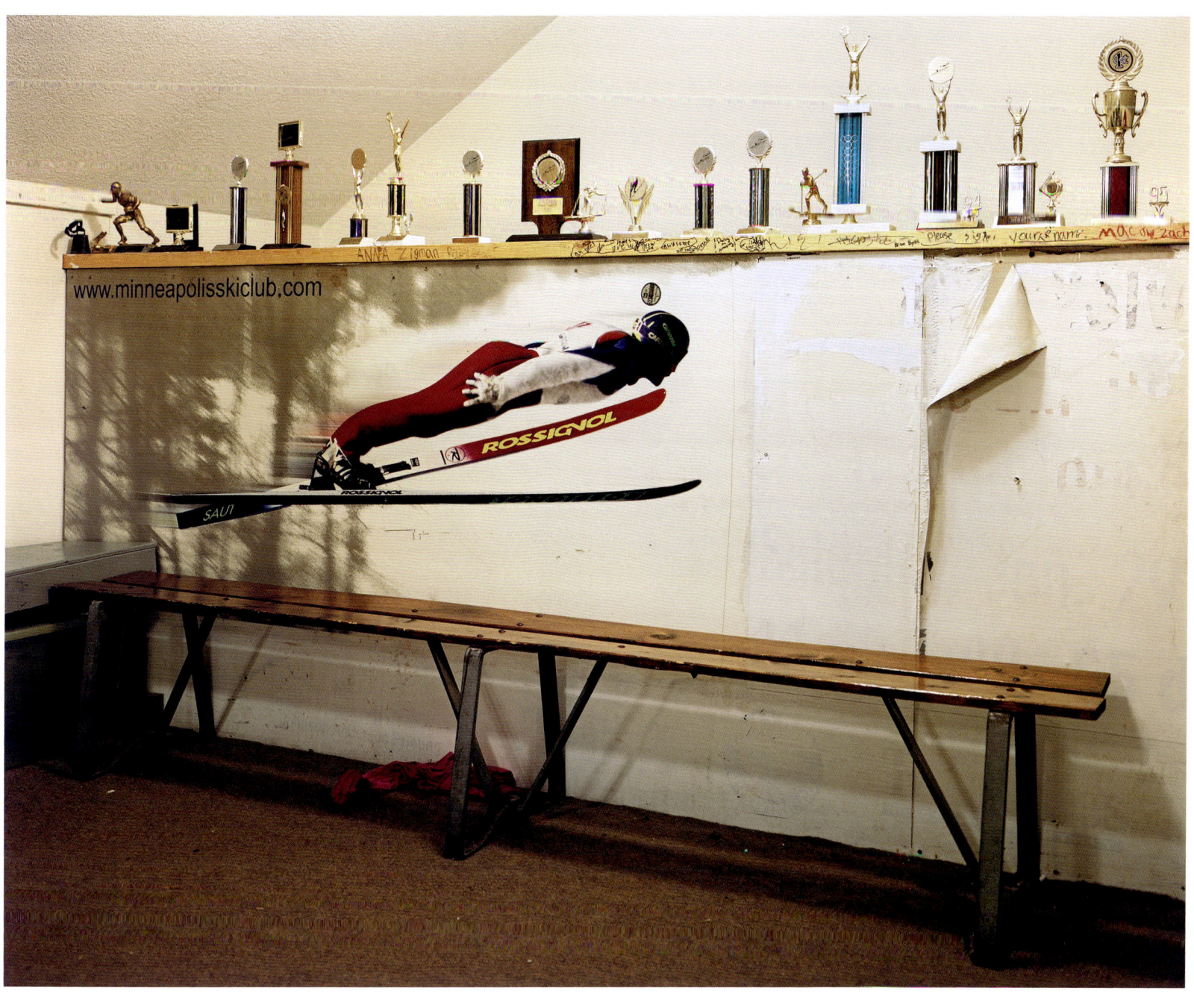

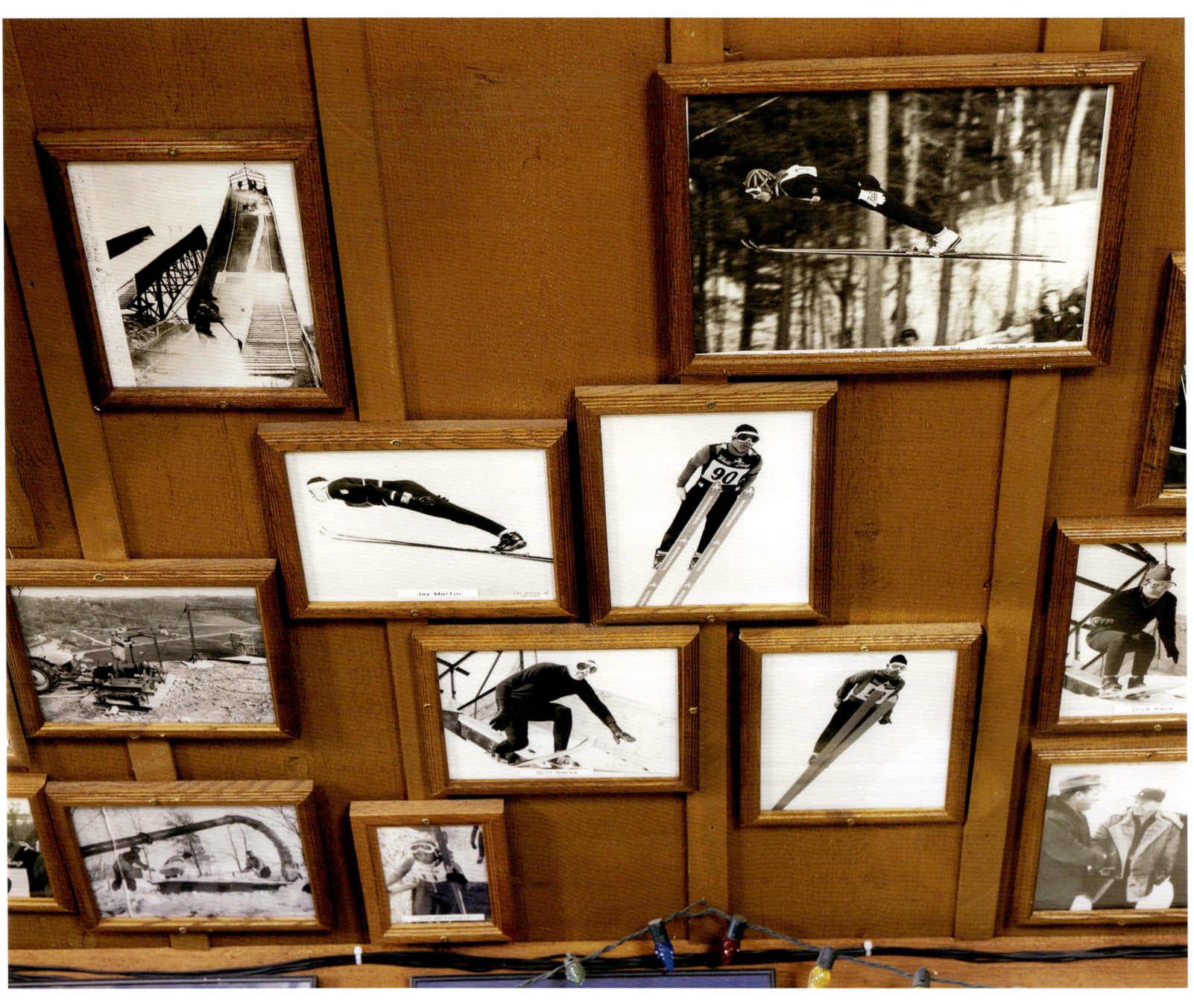

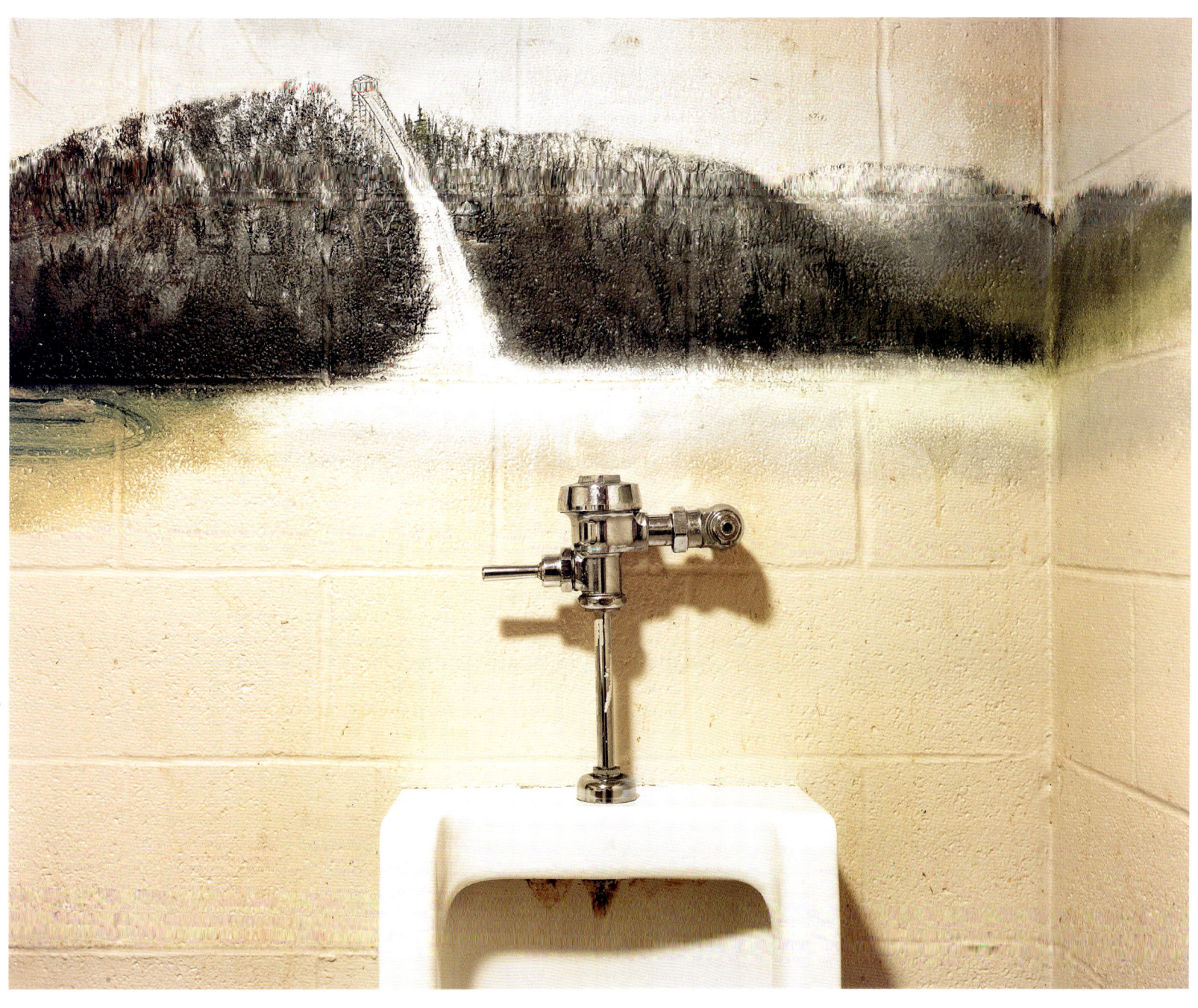

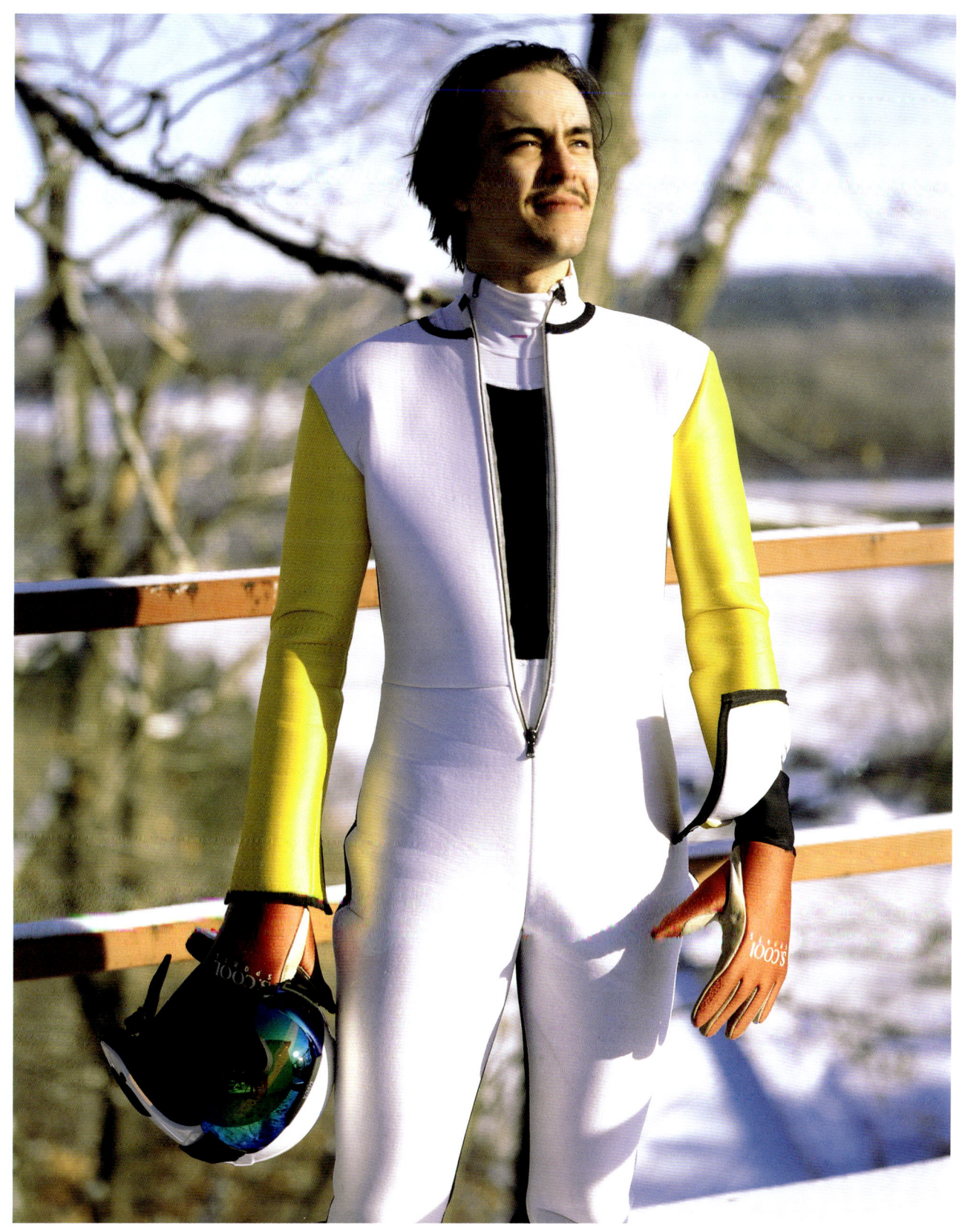

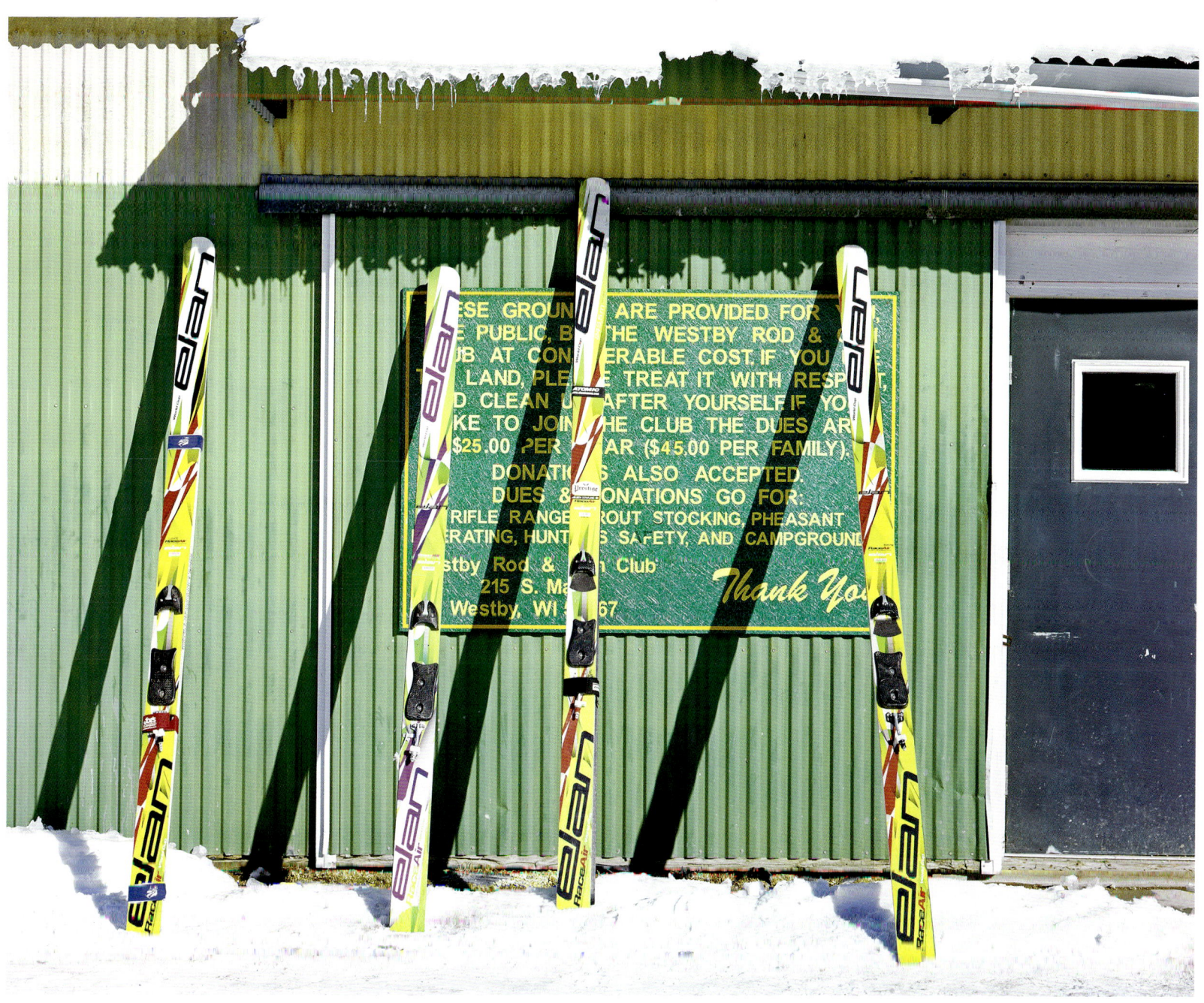

Plate List

1. Westby Sausage & Meats
2. Bush Lake, Bloomington, Minnesota
3. Silver Mine, Eau Claire, Wisconsin
4. Evan flying Norge
5. View from County Road P
6. Nik flying Bush Lake
7. Aidan, Cloquet Ski Club
8. Kindling
9. Heated beer tent
10. Elias flying Snowflake
11. Benrud Chapel, Norskedalen
12. 2016 Snowflake Royalty
13. Warm-up trailer
14. Janne and Ville, Team Finland
15. Snowflake, Westby, Wisconsin
16. Colin catching Bryce
17. Bush Lake tower
18. Mike on the startbar
19. Jorgen flying Snowflake
20. Jarle flying Snowflake
21. Aljaž flying Suicide Hill
22. Silver Mine tower
23. Hunter, Norge Ski Club
24. Anna, Blackhawk Ski Club
25. Will, Blackhawk Ski Club
26. View of the Chippewa River
27. 96th Annual Snowflake Tournament
28. Vintage Midwest flyers
29. Rod & Gun Club
30. View from Saugstad Road
31. 131st Annual Suicide Hill Tournament
32. Nick, Flying Eagles Ski Club
33. Suicide Hill, Ishpeming, Michigan
34. Norge, Fox River Grove, Illinois
35. Nate flying Silver Mine
36. 10 a.m., Marquette, Michigan
37. Leo & Leona's
38. Minneapolis ski chalet
39. Wall of fame, Snowflake Bar & Grill
40. Men's bathroom, Snowflake Bar & Grill
41. Christian, St. Paul Ski Club
42. Rod & Gun Club exterior

Reflections on the Ghosts of Place:
A Phenomenological Approach to Ski Jumping

By Chris Lamb

In mid-autumn when the leaves become vibrant reds and yellows and the air is cool and crisp, I am periodically visited by a ghost of my past. It is not a typical ghost, and, unlike Michael Mayerfield Bell's description of the ghosts of place[1], it is not tied to one particular location. This ghost is evoked by the subtle changes in the landscape that we often associate with this time of year. It is best characterized as residing on the air, a ghost of the coming of winter and the farewell of summer, evoked by the cooling temperatures, sweet-smelling forests, and cold autumn rain. Being conjured by such sensual experiences, it is for me an embodied ghost, a multiplicity of sensations and memories engrained deep within my being. As Bell observes, the ghosts of place are not only ghosts of the dead, but also ghosts of the living, and such living ghosts are the remnants of past lives preserved somehow in the present.

From the age of six to the age of twenty-four, I dedicated my life to the sport of ski jumping, or what I prefer to think of as the art of flight. While my early years as an athlete were less structured and I was less cognizant of the pursuit I was engaging in, the last twelve years of my career were regimented and intense. They were filled with a passion so deep that a day rarely went by without an hour or two of visualization or physical repetitions of my ski jumping technique. Each day was dedicated to molding my own body, from muscle to bone to mind, to become a human bird with six-foot-long skis for wings and a neoprene-suit body. Strength training was a mixture of power and technique: squats, plyometrics, hurdles, sprints were all geared toward a specific physical attainment of speed, power, and balance, yet also demanding technical movements that would assure correct positioning on the ramp and in the air. Because weight is a key factor in competitive ski jumping, my conditioning even included the things I was putting into my body (and more importantly what I was not putting into my body). Thirty-minute jogs before breakfast and after dinner, coupled with minimal caloric intake, assured a bird-like frame: 6 feet tall, 127 pounds, and ready to fly.

The cool air in the fall marks the transition from summer conditioning to the winter competition season, a moment of great anticipation when we wait to experience the fruits of our labor, or to be reminded that there is still work to be done. If you put in your hours and did your work during the summer months, your body is at this time in what Norwegians call "god form." It is, down to the last molecule a flying object. As in a bird of prey, all senses are heightened and attuned to a particular environment, with one goal in mind: defying (to the best of your ability) the forces of gravity to beat out your competitors for opportunities to fly even farther. For me, this time of year has always been one of great excitement. While

1 Michael Mayerfield Bell, "The Ghosts of Place," *Theory and Society*, Vol. 26, No. 6 (Dec. 1997), 813–836

skiing on the plastic summer surface suffices for training in the off-season, there is nothing quite like the glide one experiences on snow, or, better yet, the sensation of floating on icy, thick air. During this time of year my body would anticipate such sensations: the winter breeze entering the lungs, its bite on your face as you speed down the ramp, the sound of chattering skis on an ice track, the burning of muscles preparing for takeoff, the weightlessness of flight, and the vision from above. Even years later, these sensations are as poignant as they ever were.

Molding my body into the closest thing I could get to a bird, and taking the 2,500-plus jumps each year, assured that I had a keen attunement to the physical environment within which I flew. My flying locale was usually a 90- or 120-meter ski jump, and was general in the sense that each ski jump is built within a certain set of requirements. But each jump is also unique and specific, and therefore this place where my ghost resides is, in a sense, also a ghost of many places. It is at the ski jumping complex in Lake Placid, New York, but also that of Trondheim, Norway; Kranj, Slovenia; Sapporo, Japan; and Brattleboro, Vermont. It is in the multitude of gyms across the globe where I continued to perfect my technique, the echoing sound of squeaking shoes on wood floors, the weight of the barbell. It is at the Blackwater ski area down the road from my house in Andover, New Hampshire, where I took my first jumps at the age of six; it is on the roads of Zakopane, Poland, in Oberwiesenthal, Germany. It is in the faces of everyone with whom I have shared this journey.

In the fall, when I go for a jog through the woods and my body warms from the increased blood flow, my muscles are engaged, and I feel the refreshing embrace of the frigid air upon my face, it is as if this ghost, almost out of nowhere, inhabits my body and mind and brings me back into that world of human flight.

Chris Lamb is a New Hampshire native and former USA Ski Jumping team member. He ski jumped competitively for nearly twenty years, seven of which were spent on the international circuit, and he continues to fly for fun when possible. Chris holds a BA in environmental studies, philosophy, and literature from Marlboro College and is pursuing an MA in English at the University of Idaho.

Acknowledgments

With a few exceptions, all images were made on the Midwest Tour between 2016 and 2019.

This book came to be through the support of many, many individuals both on and off the hill. I'm especially grateful to my family for their encouragement and guidance over the years.

Thank you: Peter Geye for your wonderful essay that pays homage to the long history of Midwest flying. Ursula Damm for your vision with the sequence and beautiful design. Joey Fishman for several helpful early edits. And Chris Lamb for sharing your thoughtful reflections on why jumpers jump.

Additionally I would like to thank: Elizabeth Bell, Colin Delaney, Hannah Donovan, Eric Hagfors, Genevieve Hanson, Katherine Harrison, Jeff Hastings, Jed Hinkley, Michael Itkoff, Nick Johnson & Melissa Miller, Ruth & Ken Rupp, Mike Thompson, and Greg Windsperger.

A final thank-you to the five ski clubs pictured in this book: Flying Eagles, Ishpeming, Minneapolis, Norge, and Snowflake. Thanks to all the flyers, coaches, and volunteers.

This book is dedicated to my father,
who introduced me to this strange sport.